more modern top-down knitting

24 Garments Based on Barbara G. Walker's
12 Top-Down Templates

KRISTINA McGOWAN

PHOTOGRAPHS BY ANNA WILLIAMS

STC CRAFT | A MELANIE FALICK BOOK   NEW YORK

For my mother and father

Published in 2013 by Stewart, Tabori & Chang
An imprint of ABRAMS

Library of Congress Control Number: 2013935999

ISBN: 978-1-61769-033-4

Editor: Melanie Falick
Designer: Anna Christian
Production Manager: Tina Cameron

The text of this book was composed in Tribute and Neutraface.

Printed and bound in China

10 9 8 7 6 5 4 3 2 1

Stewart, Tabori & Chang books are available at special discounts when purchased in quantity
for premiums and promotions as well as fundraising or educational use. Special editions
can also be created to specification. For details, contact specialsales@abramsbooks.com
or the address below.

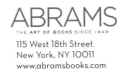

ABRAMS
THE ART OF BOOKS SINCE 1949
115 West 18th Street
New York, NY 10011
www.abramsbooks.com

contents

introduction

One morning several years ago, as I climbed up and out of New York City's Union Square subway station, I turned on my iPod to listen to Rufus Wainwright's album *Want One*. As he sang "I Don't Know What It Is," a song that begins with the hopeful line "I don't know what it is, but you've got to do it," I experienced one of those unexpected and affirmative moments—the sun shone brightly and (no joke) a flock of birds rose up and flew away to my left and right, parting as I walked through the square. (They were pigeons, not doves, but for New York City, it was my moment of idyllic inspiration.)

Wainwright's lyric, and its inherent sense of optimism, comes to mind when I think of the items I knitted for this book. The encouraging notion that "you've got to do it" has often inspired me to dismiss overly cautious reservations; it's given me strength to work tirelessly and to believe (naively or not) that, creatively, anything is possible. Ever since I was a child, knitting has been the "It" that I've been compelled to pursue. And it was in New York that I first began studying Barbara Walker's seminal 1972 technique book, *Knitting from the Top*. Walker's book became, and has remained, a welcome and beautiful reminder for me to stay curious and adventurous in life.

In the book, Walker, one of our country's most brilliant and prolific knitters, outlines twelve basic designs or templates (sweaters, skirts, hats, capes, and pants) and—with advice, diagrams, and innovative construction tips— shows how these items can be knitted from the top down (as opposed to the usual bottom up). And although non-knitters may ask (as many of my non-knitter friends have), "What's the difference between top down and bottom up?," knitters who know Walker's work and implement her ideas understand that knitting from the top down simply makes all aspects of sweater construction easier and more refined. It allows you to try on items at any point in the process and adjust the fit with ease (an advantage not to be sneezed at), and it allows you to embrace knitting's fluid art, to create continuous pieces of work and avoid the laborious task of sewing separate pieces together. In short, the top-down method takes the cake.

Technique books in knitting are rare (at least ones that outline entirely new methods) and reading Walker's work turned everything I knew about knitting on its head, presenting me with new and efficient ways of doing everything. I spent several weeks scribbling notes and dog-earing pages and working through the steps Walker outlines with needles and yarn in hand. Eventually, the lessons I learned prompted me to write my first book of knitting patterns, *Modern Top-Down Knitting*, published in the fall of 2010. So much about writing that first book was rewarding, but what will always make it special was that it provided me the excuse to travel to meet Walker at her home in Florida. Before I began working and writing, I had the chance to talk to her about her life and how she had always approached knitting with a watchful eye and a desire to make the techniques she learned better and easier.

For Walker, the "you've got to do it" spirit had moved her to always think critically of traditional knitting procedures, and her willingness to question conventions sowed many creative seeds in my brain that began to flower after I returned to New York. In many ways, the patterns that I put together in *Modern Top-Down Knitting* were the result of the unbridled sense of enthusiasm and discovery she inspired in me. Walker's ideas made me feel as if I could create any silhouette I imagined from the top down. As I flipped through magazines or saw hats, sweaters, or dresses in stores or on the people around me, I would think of Walker's templates and work out in my mind which ones could be used to make them. A favorite was Walker's set-in sleeve template, which I found elegant and versatile and used to make many of the garments for my first book. Even as I was putting my first collection together, however, I realized that I was barely scratching the surface of the rich variety of items Walker's book could help me design.

When my editor approached me to write a second book, I decided to take a more disciplined approach and systematically go through Walker's book and make garments using all twelve of her templates, designing two items from each. Indeed, I began to think of each pair of items as a private challenge. As a fan of the design competition television show *Project Runway*, I thought how much fun it might be to think of my book in similar terms. So I approached each of Walker's twelve templates as personal design challenges, and liked the idea that doing so might inspire other knitters to try the same.

To prepare, I filled in the gaps of my knitting library and ordered Walker's entire knitting catalog from Schoolhouse Press. I was especially eager to complete my set of her Stitch Pattern Treasury (a four-volume set that includes hundreds of unique stitch patterns and, often, Walker's descriptions of them). My plan was to use stitch patterns exclusively from these books and to make the entire enterprise as Walkeresque as possible. As it turned out, in many cases Walker's vignettes of certain stitch patterns were what made me want to include them. Who could resist trying a stitch pattern that was used in a vest worn by King Charles I of England on the day of his execution in 1649?

Not I! I found such details very appealing, and—especially in the case of the King Charles Brocade, which finds its way into my Robin's Egg Tunic (page 117)—they made the entire creative process far more meaningful and exciting.

My private-challenge approach allowed me to consider and embrace templates that I didn't use the first time around, like knitted pants. Every time I read through Walker's pants template I marveled at their (entirely seamless!) construction, yet developing a design for a modern-day pair threw me. I admired the finely knit, machine-made versions I saw in magazines and runway shows, but their success seemed dependent on a very fine gauge, and for hand knitting, creating such a large item on tiny needles was impractical. While working a variety of soft wools in a slightly larger gauge, however, I began to realize that my mistake was thinking of knitted pants solely as streetwear. The yarn made me think of a favorite blanket (the one that appears on popcorn-and-movie nights) and soon I was thinking of comfortable loungewear—a trusty pair of sweatpants or shorts that you'd wear on a lazy weekend while making pancakes and strong coffee. With that new perspective, the design began to make sense. With a cozy yarn, I could easily envision a wearable, go-to garment and still highlight the template's marvelous technical features.

In such cases especially, my project forced me to persevere and, ultimately, realize again how applicable and helpful Walker's ideas are in creating modern-day knitwear. Not only did my knitted pants become a favorite among my friends, one of the sweaters I designed with the dropped-shoulder template (Fox in the Snow, page 129) ended up being one of the most rewarding design experiences I have ever had. My misgivings about dropped shoulders stemmed initially from their prevalence in my 1980s high school wardrobe, and I worried that anything I created would be too boxy or feel dated. But, because this was my own version of *Project Runway*, Walker's written text became my eleventh-hour consultation with Tim Gunn. And what turned the dropped shoulder around for me, and quickly, was Walker's simple, encouraging advice to "give your imagination free rein." Charged by those simple words, I soon began thinking of the sweater's body as a canvas upon which to realize a section of one of my favorite paintings, Winslow Homer's *Fox Hunt*. I spent several days charting out its likeness and experimenting with knit and purl stitches to add texture and depth. What fun those all-nighters were creating the fox chart. I felt that I was always teetering right on the edge of creating a crazy Christmas sweater—and yet, I knew whatever the outcome, nothing that delightful could possibly go wrong.

What I present and share with you here are the twenty-four patterns that came out of my two-year journey studying and designing with Walker's twelve templates. These pages illustrate many months of my life and a great deal of hard work and joy. My hope is that my experiences, and the results of my twelve private challenges, might inspire you in your own work to discover, in Rufus Wainwright's words, the "it" you've "got to do," and do it with joyful abandon.

the projects

snow raglan

I created this raglan using the reversible boat neckline variation of Walker's classic raglan template. Be Sweet's Bambino yarn reminds me of crisp, bright snow, and so I worked elongated snowflakes using one of Walker's beautiful openwork stitch patterns (the Brisket Cable from her *Second Treasury of Knitting Patterns*).

ABBREVIATIONS

T1R: Slip next 2 sts to cn, hold to back, k1, slip last st from cn back to left-hand needle, p1, k1 from cn.

T1L: Slip next 2 sts to cn, hold to front, k1, slip last st from cn back to left-hand needle, p1, k1 from cn.

STITCH PATTERN

Brisket Cable in the Rnd
(panel of 13 sts; 10-rnd repeat)

RND 1 AND ALL ODD-NUMBERED RNDS: P2, k1, p1, k5, p1, k1, p2.

RNDS 2, 4, AND 6: P2, k1-tbl, p1, k1-tbl, yo, sk2p, yo, k1-tbl, p1, k1-tbl, p2.

RND 8: P2, T1R, k1-tbl, k1, k1-tbl, T1L, p2.

RND 10: P2, k1-tbl, p1, yo, ssk, k1, k2tog, yo, p1, k1-tbl, p2.

Repeat Rnds 1–10 for Brisket Cable in the Rnd.

Brisket Cable Flat
(panel of 13 sts; 10-row repeat)

ROW 1 AND ALL WS ROWS (WS): K2, p1, k1, p5, k1, p1, k2.

ROWS 2, 4, AND 6: P2, k1-tbl, p1, k1-tbl, yo, sk2p, yo, k1-tbl, p1, k1-tbl, p2.

ROW 8: P2, T1R, k1-tbl, k1, k1-tbl, T1L, p2.

ROW 10: P2, k1-tbl, p1, yo, ssk, k1, k2tog, yo, p1, k1-tbl, p2.

Repeat Rows 1–10 for Brisket Cable Flat.

sizes

X-Small (Small, Medium, Large, 1X-Large, 2X-Large, 3X-Large)

finished measurements

29 1/2 (33 1/2, 37 1/2, 41 1/2, 45 1/2, 49 1/2, 53 1/2)" bust

Note: This yarn has quite a bit of give. For a close fit, select a size 4-5" smaller than your bust measurements.

yarn

Be Sweet Bambino (70% organic cotton / 30% bamboo; 97 yards / 50 grams): 6 (7, 8, 8, 9, 10, 11) balls #890 White

needles

One 24" (60 cm) long or longer circular (circ) needle size US 7 (4.5 mm)

Change needle size if necessary to obtain correct gauge.

notions

Cable needle; stitch markers

gauge

16 sts and 24 rows = 4" (10 cm) in Reverse Stockinette stitch (Rev St st)

YOKE

CO 41 (43, 45, 47, 49, 49, 51) sts for Front, pm, 13 sts for Left Sleeve, pm, 41 (43, 45, 47, 49, 49, 51) sts for Back, pm, and 13 sts for Right Sleeve—108 (112, 116, 120, 124, 124, 128) sts. Join for working in the rnd, being careful not to twist sts; pm for beginning of rnd.

NEXT RND: [P1 (2, 3, 4, 5, 5, 6), work Brisket Cable in the Rnd over 39 sts, p1 (2, 3, 4, 5, 5, 6), sm, work Brisket Cable in the Rnd to next marker, sm] twice.

Shape Raglan

Note: The first marker slipped in Increase Rnds is the beginning-of-rnd marker; make sure that the first increase, which is for the Right Sleeve, is worked before that marker is slipped.

INCREASE RND 1: Continuing to work Brisket Cables as established, and remaining sts in Rev St st, increase 8 sts this rnd, then every other rnd 17 (18, 19, 18, 17, 16, 15) times, as follows: [M1-p-R, sm, p1, M1-p-L, work to 1 st before marker, M1-p-R, p1, sm, M1-p-L, work to marker] twice—252 (264, 276, 272, 268, 260, 256) sts [77 (81, 85, 85, 85, 83, 83) sts each for Front and Back; 49 (51, 53, 51, 49, 47, 45) sts each Sleeve]. Work even for 1 rnd.

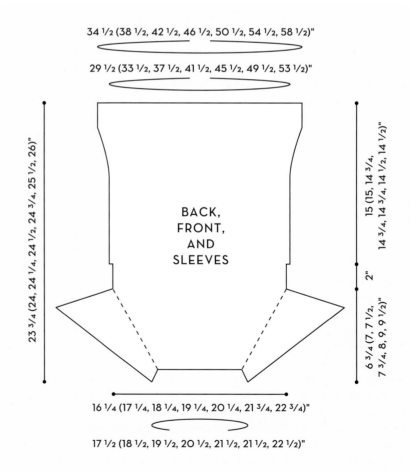

34 ½ (38 ½, 42 ½, 46 ½, 50 ½, 54 ½, 58 ½)"

29 ½ (33 ½, 37 ½, 41 ½, 45 ½, 49 ½, 53 ½)"

BACK, FRONT, AND SLEEVES

23 ¾ (24, 24 ¼, 24 ½, 24 ¾, 25 ½, 26)"

15 (15, 14 ¾, 14 ¾, 14 ¾, 14 ½, 14 ½)"

2"

6 ¾ (7, 7 ½, 7 ¾, 8, 9, 9 ½)"

16 ¼ (17 ¼, 18 ¼, 19 ¼, 20 ¼, 21 ¾, 22 ¾)"

17 ½ (18 ½, 19 ½, 20 ½, 21 ½, 21 ½, 22 ½)"

SIZES LARGE, 1X-LARGE, 2X-LARGE, AND 3X-LARGE ONLY

INCREASE RND 2 (RS): Increase 8 sts this rnd, as follows: [M1-p-R, sm, p1, M1-p-L, work to 1 st before marker, M1-p-R, p1, sm, M1-p-L, work to marker] twice. Work even for 1 rnd.

INCREASE RND 3 (RS): Increase 4 sts this rnd, as follows: [Sm, p1, M1-p-L, work to 1 st before marker, M1-p-R, p1, sm, M1-p-L, work to marker] twice. Work even for 1 rnd.

Repeat last 4 rnds - (-, -, 0, 1, 3, 4) time(s)— - (-, -, 284, 292, 308, 316) sts [- (-, -, 89, 93, 99, 103) sts each Back and Front, - (-, -, 53, 53, 55, 55) sts each Sleeve].

ALL SIZES

Complete Sleeves

NEXT RND: Work to marker, BO next 49 (51, 53, 53, 53, 55, 55) sts for Left Sleeve, removing markers, join a second ball of yarn, work to marker, BO next 49 (51, 53, 53, 53, 55, 55) sts for Right Sleeve, removing markers. Working FRONT AND BACK AT THE SAME TIME using separate balls of yarn, continue working patterns as established, working Brisket Cable Flat instead of Brisket Cable in the Rnd, and beginning with row of Brisket Cable Flat after last rnd of Brisket Cable in the Rnd worked; work even until piece measures 2" from Sleeve Caps, ending with a WS row. Break yarn for Back.

BODY

Join Back to Front

NEXT ROW (RS): CO 1 (5, 9, 13, 17, 19, 23) st(s) for right underarm, work to end of Front, CO 1 (5, 9, 13, 17, 19, 23) st(s) for left underarm, work across Back to 6 sts before center right underarm st—156 (172, 188, 204, 220, 236, 252) sts. Place marker on either side of 13 sts centered on each underarm (for some sizes this will include Body sts, for other sizes, it will only include CO sts). First marker is beginning-of-rnd marker.

NEXT RND: [Work Brisket Cable in the Rnd to marker, beginning with next rnd after last row worked on Body, sm, work in patterns as established to marker (working Brisket Cable in the Rnd instead of Brisket Cable Flat, and beginning with next rnd after last row worked on Body), sm] twice. Work even until piece measures 9" from underarm.

Shape Hips

Note: The first marker slipped in the Increase Rnd is the beginning-of-rnd marker; make sure that the first increase is worked before that marker is slipped.

INCREASE RND: Increase 4 sts this rnd, then every 6 rnds 4 times as follows, working increased sts in Rev St st as they become available: [M1-p-L, sm, work to marker, sm, M1-p-R, work to marker] twice—176 (192, 208, 224, 240, 256, 272) sts. Work even until piece measures 15 (15, 14¾, 14¾, 14¾, 14½, 14½)" from underarm. BO all sts.

Weave in ends. Block as desired.

twins raglan

The merino-alpaca blend I chose for this classic raglan provides wonderful stitch definition. After I worked up a swatch of it, I decided it was the perfect base upon which to infuse color using duplicate stitch. I researched a number of Hungarian, Palestinian, and Mexican embroidery motifs and, ultimately, chose a vibrant Palestinian design that features twin lions (and nods to my own status as a twin).

To transfer the chart to your sweater, it helps to use a water-soluble fabric marker. After marking the corresponding stitches and working the duplicates, simply spray your knitting with water and the markings will disappear as if by magic. You can also create your own design on knitter's graph paper and continue as above.

STITCH PATTERN

1x1 Rib
(even number of sts; 1-rnd repeat)
ALL RNDS: *K1, p1; repeat from * to end.

YOKE

Using longer circ needle, CO 2 sts for Left Front, pm, 13 sts for Left Sleeve, pm, 37 (39, 41, 45, 47, 49) sts for Back, pm, 13 sts for Right Sleeve, pm, and 2 sts for Right Front—67 (69, 71, 75, 77, 79) sts. Purl 1 row.

Shape Neck and Raglan
INCREASE ROW 1 (RS): K1-f/b, M1-R, k1, sm, M1-L, knit to marker, M1-R, sm, k1, M1-L, knit to 1 st before marker, M1-R, k1, sm, M1-L, knit to marker, M1-R, sm, k1, M1-L, k1-f/b—77 (79, 81, 85, 87, 89) sts. Purl 1 row.

sizes

X-Small (Small, Medium, Large, 1X-Large, 2X-Large)

finished measurements

31½ (35, 39½, 44, 48½, 53)" bust

yarn

Shibui Knits Merino Alpaca (50% baby alpaca / 50% merino wool; 131 yards / 100 grams): 7 (8, 9, 9, 10, 11) hanks Ivory (MC)

Shibui Knits Staccato (70% superwash merino wool / 30% silk); 191 yards / 50 grams): 1 hank each Redwood (A), Tide (B), and Dijon (C); *Note: Only a small amount of these yarns was used; if you would prefer to substitute yarn from your stash, choose a yarn that knits up at a gauge of 28–32 sts to 4" (10 cm).*

needles

One 24" (60 cm) long or longer circular (circ) needle size US 8 (5 mm)

One 16" (40 cm) long circular needle size US 8 (5 mm)

One set of five double-pointed needles (dpn) size US 8 (5 mm)

Change needle size if necessary to obtain correct gauge.

notions

Stitch markers; water-soluble fabric marker; tapestry needle

gauge

18 sts and 24 rows = 4" (10 cm) in Stockinette stitch (St st)

INCREASE ROW 2 (RS): Increase 10 sts this row, then every other row 5 (5, 5, 6, 6, 7) times, as follows: K1-f/b, [knit to 1 st before marker, M1-R, k1, sm, M1-L, knit to marker, M1-R, sm, k1, M1-L] twice, knit to last st, k1-f/b—137 (139, 141, 155, 157, 169) sts [16 (16, 16, 18, 18, 20) sts each Front, 27 (27, 27, 29, 29, 31) sts each Sleeve, 51 (53, 55, 61, 63, 67) sts for Back. Purl 1 row.

Join Fronts

NEXT ROW (RS): CO 19 (21, 23, 25, 27, 27) sts for Front neck, [knit to 1 st before marker, M1-R, k1, sm, M1-L, knit to marker, M1-R, sm, k1, M1-L] twice, knit to end—164 (168, 172, 188, 192, 204) sts. Join for working in the rnd; pm for beginning of rnd. Knit 1 rnd.

Shape Raglan

INCREASE RND 1: Increase 8 sts this rnd, then every other rnd 8 (11, 15, 15, 17, 18) times, as follows: [Knit to 1 st before marker, M1-R, k1, sm, M1-L, knit to marker, M1-R, sm, k1, M1-L] twice, knit to end—236 (264, 300, 316, 336, 356) sts [71 (79, 89, 95, 101, 107) sts each for Front and Back, 47 (53, 61, 63, 67, 71) sts each Sleeve]. Work even for 7 (5, 1, 1, 1, 1) rnd(s).

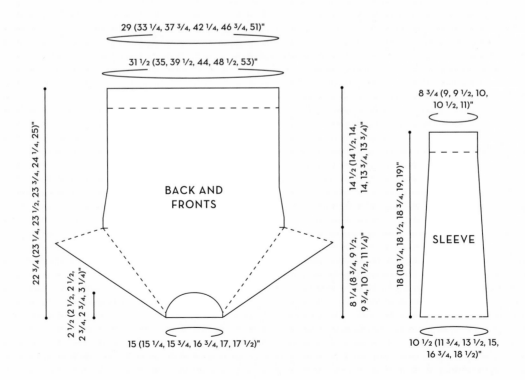

29 (33 1/4, 37 3/4, 42 1/4, 46 3/4, 51)"

31 1/2 (35, 39 1/2, 44, 48 1/2, 53)"

8 3/4 (9, 9 1/2, 10, 10 1/2, 11)"

22 3/4 (23 1/4, 23 1/2, 23 3/4, 24 1/4, 25)"

14 1/2 (14 1/2, 14, 14, 13 3/4, 13 3/4)"

BACK AND FRONTS

18 (18 1/4, 18 1/2, 18 3/4, 19, 19)"

SLEEVE

8 1/4 (8 3/4, 9 1/2, 9 3/4, 10 1/2, 11 1/4)"

2 1/2 (2 1/2, 2 1/2, 2 3/4, 2 3/4, 3 1/4)"

15 (15 1/4, 15 3/4, 16 3/4, 17, 17 1/2)"

10 1/2 (11 3/4, 13 1/2, 15, 16 3/4, 18 1/2)"

BODY

Divide for Body

NEXT RND: Knit to first marker, transfer next 47 (53, 61, 63, 67, 71) sts to waste yarn for Left Sleeve, removing markers, CO 0 (0, 0, 4, 8, 12) sts for underarm, pm for side at center of CO sts (between Front and Back for sizes XS, S, and M), knit to next marker, transfer next 47 (53, 61, 63, 67, 71) sts to waste yarn for Right Sleeve, removing markers, CO 0 (0, 0, 4, 8, 12) sts for underarm, pm for side and new beginning of rnd at center of CO sts (between Front and Back for sizes XS, S, and M)—142 (158, 178, 198, 218, 238) sts. Continuing in St st, work even for 1", ending final rnd 2 sts before beginning of next rnd.

Shape Waist

Note: Each Waist shaping rnd begins 2 sts before beginning-of-rnd marker.

DECREASE RND: Decrease 4 sts this rnd, then every 9 rnds 2 (1, 1, 1, 1, 1) time(s), working decreases on last 2 sts of rnd and first 2 sts of next rnd, as follows: [K2tog, sm, ssk, knit to 2 sts before next marker] twice, knit to end—130 (150, 170, 190, 210, 230) sts remain. Work even until piece measures 12 ½ (12 ½, 12, 12, 11 ¾, 11 ¾)" from underarm. Change to 1x1 Rib; work even for 2". BO all sts in pattern.

SLEEVES

Transfer Sleeve sts from waste yarn to shorter circ needle. With RS facing, rejoin yarn at center underarm. Pick up and knit 0 (0, 0, 2, 4, 6) sts from sts CO for underarm, knit to end, pick up and knit 0 (0, 0, 2, 4, 6) sts from sts CO for underarm—47 (53, 61, 67, 75, 83) sts. Join for working in the rnd; pm for beginning of rnd. Knit 1 rnd, ending 2 sts before beginning of rnd.

Shape Sleeve

Note: Each Sleeve shaping rnd begins 2 sts before beginning-of-rnd marker. Change to dpns when necessary for number of sts on needle.

DECREASE RND 1: Decrease 2 sts this rnd, every 40 (18, 8, 8, 6, 4) rnds 1 (2, 5, 8, 11, 4) times, then every 18 (14, 14, 12, 10, 6) rnds 2 (3, 3, 2, 2, 12) times, as follows: K2tog, sm, ssk, knit to end—39 (41, 43, 45, 47, 49) sts remain. Work even until piece measures 16 (16 ¼, 16 ½, 16 ¾, 17, 17)" from underarm, decreasing 1 st on last rnd—38 (40, 42, 44, 46, 48) sts remain.

Change to 1x1 Rib; work even for 2". BO all sts in pattern.

FINISHING

With RS facing, using shorter circ needle, and beginning at right shoulder, pick up and knit 35 (37, 39, 43, 45, 47) sts around neck edge, then 1 st in each CO st and 2 sts for every 3 rows around front neck opening. Join for working in the rnd; pm for beginning of rnd. Purl 1 rnd. BO all sts knitwise. Weave in all ends; block as desired.

Duplicate Stitch

Using 2 stands of yarn held together, work Duplicate Stitch (see page 150), following Chart. Begin Chart just below neck edging, centering Chart on center of neck, and work from neck down.

DUPLICATE STITCH CHART

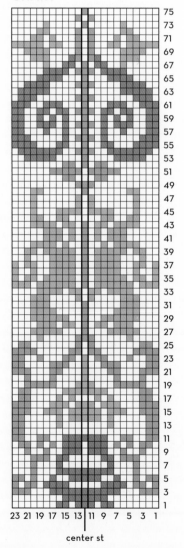

center st

KEY
■ A ■ B □ C

david cardigan

Handmade raglan cardigans always make me think of reading on rainy afternoons, and I tried to impart a similar sense of comfort and calm to this piece. Leather buttons and elbow patches harken to the 1970s of my childhood, and I call the sweater "David Cardigan" as tribute to my five favorite authors, who all happen to be named David and whose audiobooks I listened to while making the pieces for this collection (Wallace, Sedaris, Rakoff, Eggers, and Benioff).

STITCH PATTERN

2x3 Rib Flat
(multiple of 5 sts + 4; 1-row repeat)
ROW 1 (RS): K1, *k2, p3; repeat from * to last 3 sts, k3.
ROW 2: Knit the knit sts and purl the purl sts as they face you.
Repeat Row 2 for 2x3 Rib Flat.

2x3 Rib in the Rnd
(multiple of 5 sts; 1-rnd repeat)
ALL RNDS: K1, p3, *k2, p3; repeat from * to last st, k1.

YOKE

Using longer circ needle, CO 1 st for Right Front, pm, 17 (17, 17, 19, 19, 19) sts for Right Sleeve, pm, 43 (45, 47, 47, 49, 51) sts for Back, pm, 17 (17, 17, 19, 19, 19) sts for Left Sleeve, pm, and 1 st for Left Front—79 (81, 83, 87, 89, 91) sts. Purl 1 row.

Shape Raglan and Neck
INCREASE ROW 1 (RS): K1-f/b, *M1-R, sm, k1, M1-L, knit to 1 st before marker, M1-R, k1, sm, M1-L*, knit to marker; repeat from * to *, k1-f/b—89 (91, 93, 97, 99, 101) sts. Purl 1 row.

X-Small (Small, Medium, Large, 1X-Large, 2X-Large)

finished measurements
32 1/2 (36 1/2, 40 1/2, 44 1/2, 48 1/2, 52 1/2)" bust, buttoned

yarn
Rowan Yarns Lima (84% baby alpaca / 8% merino wool / 8% nylon; 120 yards / 50 grams): 11 (12, 13, 15, 16, 17) balls Puno

needles
One 29" (70 cm) long or longer circular (circ) needle size US 9 (5.5 mm)

One 16" (40 cm) long circular needle size US 9 (5.5 mm)

One set of five double-pointed needles (dpn) size US 9 (5.5 mm)

Change needle size if necessary to obtain correct gauge.

notions
Stitch markers; 2 removable st markers; waste yarn; seven ¾" leather buttons; sewing needle and matching thread; 2 oval leather elbow patches 5½" long x 4" wide, or one piece of leather at least 5½" x 8"; leather punch

gauge
20 sts and 27 rows = 4" (10 cm) in Stockinette stitch (St st)

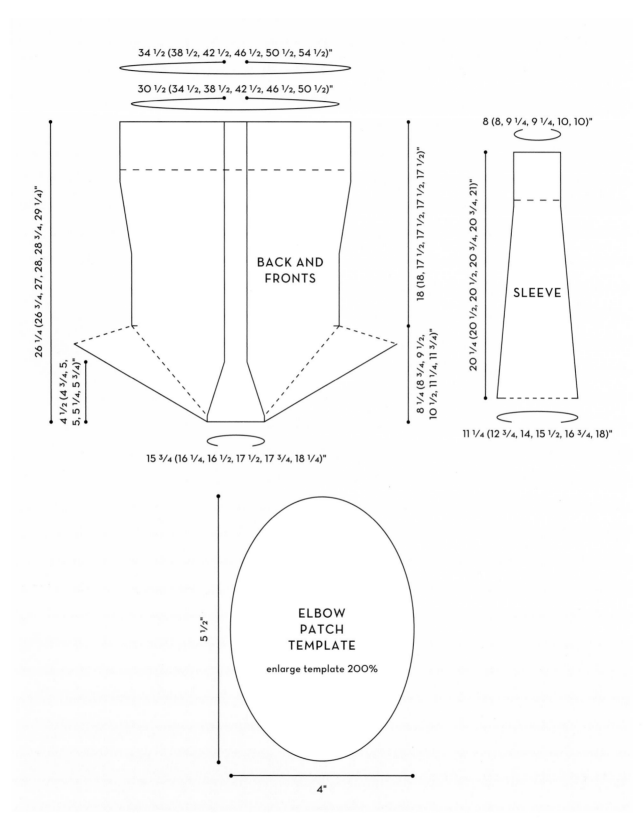

34 1/2 (38 1/2, 42 1/2, 46 1/2, 50 1/2, 54 1/2)"

30 1/2 (34 1/2, 38 1/2, 42 1/2, 46 1/2, 50 1/2)"

BACK AND FRONTS

26 1/4 (26 3/4, 27, 28, 28 3/4, 29 1/4)"

18 (18, 17 1/2, 17 1/2, 17 1/2, 17 1/2)"

4 1/2 (4 3/4, 5, 5, 5 1/4, 5 3/4)"

8 1/4 (8 3/4, 9 1/2, 10 1/2, 11 1/4, 11 3/4)"

15 3/4 (16 1/4, 16 1/2, 17 1/2, 17 3/4, 18 1/4)"

8 (8, 9 1/4, 9 1/4, 10, 10)"

SLEEVE

20 1/4 (20 1/2, 20 1/2, 20 3/4, 20 3/4, 21)"

11 1/4 (12 3/4, 14, 15 1/2, 16 3/4, 18)"

ELBOW
PATCH
TEMPLATE

enlarge template 200%

5 1/2"

4"

INCREASE ROW 2 (RS): Increase 10 sts this row, then every other row 13 (14, 15, 15, 16, 17) times, as follows: K1-f/b, [knit to marker, M1-R, sm, k1, M1-L, knit to 1 st before marker, M1-R, k1, sm, M1-L] twice, knit to last st, k1-f/b —229 (241, 253, 257, 269, 281) sts [31 (33, 35, 35, 37, 39) sts each Front, 47 (49, 51, 53, 55, 57) sts each Sleeve, 73 (77, 81, 81, 85, 89) sts for Back]. Purl 1 row.

Shape Raglan

INCREASE ROW 3 (RS): Increase 8 sts this row, then every other row 3 (6, 5, 4, 3, 2) times, as follows: [Knit to marker, M1-R, sm, k1, M1-L, knit to 1 st before marker, M1-R, k1, sm, M1-L] twice, knit to end—261 (297, 301, 297, 301, 305) sts [35 (40, 41, 40, 41, 42) sts each Front, 55 (63, 63, 63, 63, 63) sts each Sleeve (including 2 raglan column sts), 81 (91, 93, 91, 93, 95) sts for Back]. Work even for 5 (1, 1, 1, 1, 1) row(s).

SIZES MEDIUM, LARGE, 1X-LARGE, AND 2X-LARGE ONLY

INCREASE ROW 4 (RS): Repeat Increase Row 3. Purl 1 row.

INCREASE ROW 5 (RS): Increase 4 sts this row, as follows: [Knit to marker, M1-R, sm, knit to next marker, sm, M1-L] twice, knit to end. Purl 1 row.

Repeat last 4 rows - (-, 0, 2, 3, 4) times— - (-, 313, 333, 349, 365) sts [- (-, 43, 46, 49, 52) sts each Front, - (-, 65, 69, 71, 73) sts each Sleeve, - (-, 97, 103, 109, 115) sts for Back].

ALL SIZES

BODY

Divide for Body

NEXT ROW (RS): Knit to first marker, remove marker, transfer next 55 (63, 65, 69, 71, 73) sts to waste yarn for Left Sleeve, removing markers, CO 1 (1, 5, 9, 13, 17) st(s) for underarm, place removable marker for side on center st of CO sts (move marker up as you work), knit to next marker, remove marker, transfer next 55 (63, 65, 69, 71, 73) sts to waste yarn for Right Sleeve, removing markers, CO 1 (1, 5, 9, 13, 17) st(s) for underarm, place removable marker for side on center st of CO sts, knit to end—153 (173, 193, 213, 233, 253) sts remain. Continuing in St st, work even until piece measures 6" from underarm, ending with a WS row.

Shape Hip

INCREASE ROW (RS): Increase 4 sts this row, then every 12 rows 4 times, as follows: [Knit to marked st, M1-R, k1 (marked st), M1-L] twice, knit to end—173 (193, 213, 233, 253, 273) sts. Work even until piece measures 14 (14, 13½, 13½, 13½, 13½)" from underarm, ending with a WS row, decrease 4 sts on last row—169 (189, 209, 229, 249, 269) sts remain. Change to 2x3 Rib; work even for 4". BO all sts in pattern.

SLEEVES

Transfer Sleeve sts from waste yarn to shorter circ needle. With RS facing, rejoin yarn at center underarm. Pick up and knit 1 (1, 3, 5, 7, 9) st(s) from sts CO for underarm, work to end, pick up and knit 0 (0, 2, 4, 6, 8) sts from sts CO for underarm—56 (64, 70, 78, 84, 90) sts. Join for working in the rnd;

pm for beginning of rnd. Continuing in St st, work even until piece measures 1" from underarm, ending final rnd 2 sts before beginning of next rnd.

Shape Sleeve

Note: Each Sleeve shaping rnd begins 2 sts before beginning-of-rnd marker.
Change to dpns when necessary for number of sts on needle.

DECREASE RND: Decrease 2 sts this rnd, every 14 (10, 10, 8, 6, 6) rnds 4 (3, 3, 3, 16, 10) times, then every 12 (8, 8, 6, 0, 4) rnds 3 (8, 8, 12, 0, 9) times, working decreases on last 2 sts of rnd and first 2 sts of next rnd, as follows: K2tog, sm, ssk—40 (40, 46, 46, 50, 50) sts remain. Work even until piece measures 16 ¼ (16 ½, 16 ½, 16 ¼, 16 ¾, 17)" from underarm, and decreasing 0 (0, 1, 1, 0, 0) st(s) on final rnd—40 (40, 45, 45, 50, 50) sts remain. Change to 2x3 Rib in the Rnd; work even for 4". BO all sts in pattern.

FINISHING

Neckband

With RS facing, using larger circ needle and beginning at lower Right Front edge, pick up and knit 88 (90, 90, 92, 94, 94) sts along Right Front to base of neck shaping, pm, 44 (45, 46, 46, 47, 48) sts to beginning of Right Sleeve, 1 st in each CO st to end of Left Sleeve, 44 (45, 46, 46, 47, 48) sts to base of neck shaping, pm, then 88 (90, 90, 92, 94, 94) sts along Left Front. Knit 1 row.

INCREASE ROW (RS): Increase 4 sts this row, then every other row twice, as follows: [Knit to 1 st before marker, M1-R, k1, sm, M1-L] twice, knit to end. Knit 1 row.

BIND-OFF ROW (RS): Knit to marker, bind off to next marker, knit to end.

Left Front Band

Working on Left Front Band only, knit 10 rows. BO all sts purlwise.

Right Front Band

Place markers along Right Front for 7 buttonholes, the first ½" from lower edge of neckband, the last ½" from top edge of neckband, and the remaining 5 evenly spaced between. With WS facing, rejoin yarn to remaining sts for Right Front Band. Knit 1 row.

BUTTONHOLE ROW (RS): [Knit to marker, yo, k2tog] 7 times, knit to end. Knit 8 rows. BO all sts purlwise.

Block as desired.

Elbow Patches

If you bought pre-made elbow patches with punched holes, pin patches in desired location, then sew to sweater. If you prefer to make your own, photocopy template, enlarging it 200% (it should measure 5 ½" long x 4" wide), then use template to cut out 2 pieces of leather; punch holes approximately every ¼", ¼" in from edge. Pin in desired location, then sew to sweater using backstitch.

Sew on buttons opposite buttonholes. Weave in all ends. Block as desired.

softest stripe cardigan

I made this cardigan by combining linen yarn with a soft, muted gray mohair. For the stripes, the mohair helped tone down the bright, almost neon orange linen, but allowed just a hint of brightness to remain. The result is one of the softest sweaters I have ever made and one that is heavenly to wear.

STITCH PATTERNS

Stripe Pattern

(any number of sts; 8-row/rnd repeat)

*Working in St st, work 4 rows/rnds with 1 strand each of B and C held together, then 4 rows/rnds with 1 strand each of A and B held together; repeat from * for Stripe Pattern.

1x1 Rib Flat

(odd number of sts; 1-row repeat)

ROW 1 (RS): K1, *p1, k1; repeat from * to end.

ROW 2: Knit the knit sts and purl the purl sts as they face you.

Repeat Row 2 for 1x1 Rib Flat.

1x1 Rib in the Rnd

(even number of sts; 1-rnd repeat)

ALL RNDS: *K1, p1; repeat from * to end.

SPECIAL TECHNIQUE

Jogless Color Change: To minimize the jog where colors change when working stripes in-the-round, work one round with the new color, slip beginning-of-the round marker, slip the first stitch of the next round to the right-hand needle purlwise, then continue knitting.

sizes

Small (Medium, Large, 1X-Large, 2X-Large, 3X-Large)

finished measurements

35 ¼ (39 ¼, 43 ¼, 47 ¼, 51 ¼, 55 ¼)" bust, buttoned

yarn

Shibui Knits Linen (100% linen; 246 yards / 50 grams): 4 (5, 5, 5, 6, 6) hanks Ash (A); 2 hanks Poppy (C)

Shibui Knits Silk Cloud (60% kid mohair / 40% silk; 330 yards / 25 grams): 4 (4, 5, 5, 5, 6) hanks Ash (B)

needles

One 29" (70 cm) long or longer circular (circ) needle size US 7 (4.5 mm)

One 16" (40 cm) long circular needle size US 7 (4.5 mm)

One set of five double-pointed needles (dpn) size US 7 (4.5 mm)

Change needle size if necessary to obtain correct gauge.

notions

Crochet hook size US E/4 (3.5 mm); waste yarn; stitch markers; seven ½" buttons

gauge

24 sts and 32 rows = 4" (10 cm) in Stockinette stitch (St st), using 1 strand each of A and B held together

Simple crochet stitches provide a clean finish for knitted items. For this cardigan, I worked a smooth, sturdy button band with several rows of single crochet.

YOKE

Using 1 strand each of A and B held together, CO 1 st for Left Front, pm, 16 (16, 16, 18, 18, 18) sts for Left Sleeve, pm, 42 (44, 46, 46, 48, 50) sts for Back, pm, 16 (16, 16, 18, 18, 18) sts for Right Sleeve, pm, and 1 st for Right Front—76 (78, 80, 84, 86, 88) sts. Purl 1 row.

Shape Neck and Raglan

INCREASE ROW 1 (RS): K1-f/b, *M1-R, sm, k1, M1-L, knit to 1 st before marker, M1-R, k1, sm, M1-L*, knit to marker; repeat from * to *, k1-f/b—86 (88, 90, 94, 96, 98) sts. Purl 1 row.

INCREASE ROW 2 (RS): Increase 10 sts this row, then every other row 13 (14, 15, 15, 16, 17) times, as follows: K1-f/b, [knit to marker, M1-R, sm, k1, M1-L, knit to 1 st before marker, M1-R, k1, sm, M1-L] twice, knit to last st, k1-f/b—226 (238, 250, 254, 266, 278) sts [31 (33, 35, 35, 37, 39) sts each Front; 46 (48, 50, 52, 54, 56) sts each Sleeve; 72 (76, 80, 80, 84, 88) sts for Back]. Purl 1 row.

Shape Raglan and Begin Stripe Pattern

Note: Yoke shaping and Stripe Pattern are worked at the same time; please read entire section through before beginning.

INCREASE ROW 3 (RS): Increase 8 sts this row, then every other row 17 (16, 16, 12, 13, 10) times, as follows: [Knit to marker, M1-R, sm, k1, M1-L, knit to 1 st before marker, M1-R, k1, sm, M1-L] twice, knit to end—370 (374, 386, 358, 378, 366) sts [49 (50, 52, 48, 51, 50) sts each Front; 82 (82, 84, 78, 82, 78) sts each Sleeve; 108 (110, 114, 106, 112, 110) sts for Back]. Purl 1 row. AT THE SAME TIME, when piece measures 6 (6½, 7¼, 7¾, 8¾, 9¼)" from the beginning, ending with a WS row, change to Stripe Pattern.

SIZES MEDIUM, LARGE, 1X-LARGE, 2X-LARGE, AND 3X-LARGE ONLY

INCREASE ROW 4 (RS): Repeat Increase Row 3. Purl 1 row.

INCREASE ROW 5 (RS): Increase 4 sts this row, as follows: [Knit to marker, M1-R, sm, knit to next marker, sm, M1-L] twice, knit to end. Purl 1 row.

Repeat last 4 rows - (0, 1, 4, 5, 7) time(s)— - (386, 410, 418, 450, 462) sts [- (52, 56, 58, 63, 66) sts each Front, - (84, 88, 88, 94, 94) sts each Sleeve, - (114, 122, 126, 136, 142) sts for Back].

BODY

Divide for Body

NEXT ROW (RS): Knit to first marker, transfer next 82 (84, 88, 88, 94, 94) sts to waste yarn for Left Sleeve, removing markers, CO 0 (6, 10, 18, 20, 26) sts for underarm, pm for side at center of CO sts (between Front and Back for size S), knit to next marker, CO 0 (6, 10, 18, 20, 26) sts for underarm, pm for side at center of CO sts, knit to end—206 (230, 254, 278, 302, 326) sts. Continuing to work Stripe Pattern until you have 10 contrasting color stripes, and changing to 1 strand each of A and B held together when Stripe Pattern is complete, work even until piece measures 7½" from underarm, ending with a WS row.

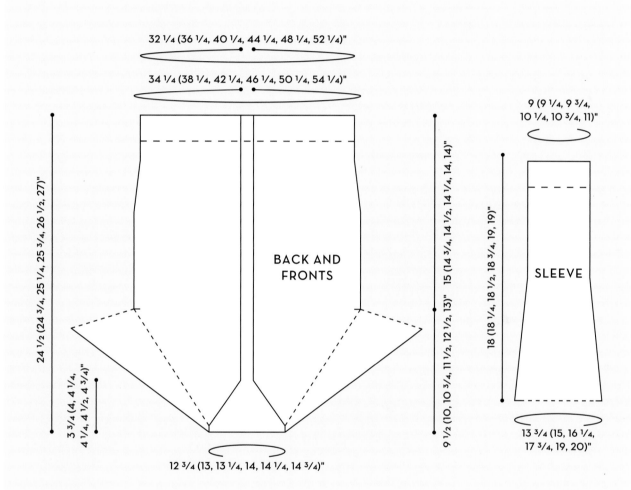

32 1/4 (36 1/4, 40 1/4, 44 1/4, 48 1/4, 52 1/4)"

34 1/4 (38 1/4, 42 1/4, 46 1/4, 50 1/4, 54 1/4)"

9 (9 1/4, 9 3/4, 10 1/4, 10 3/4, 11)"

24 1/2 (24 3/4, 25 1/4, 25 3/4, 26 1/2, 27)"

BACK AND FRONTS

15 (14 3/4, 14 1/2, 14 1/4, 14, 14)"

18 (18 1/4, 18 1/2, 18 3/4, 19, 19)"

SLEEVE

3 3/4 (4, 4 1/4, 4 1/4, 4 1/2, 4 3/4)"

9 1/2 (10, 10 3/4, 11 1/2, 12 1/2, 13)"

12 3/4 (13, 13 1/4, 14, 14 1/4, 14 3/4)"

13 3/4 (15, 16 1/4, 17 3/4, 19, 20)"

Shape Hips

DECREASE ROW (RS): Decrease 4 sts this row, then every 16 rows twice, as follows: [Knit to 2 sts before marker, ssk, sm, k2tog] twice, knit to end—194 (218, 242, 266, 290, 314) sts remain. Work even until piece measures 13 (12¾, 12½, 12¼, 12, 12)" from underarm, ending with a WS row, decreasing 1 st on last row—193 (217, 241, 265, 289, 313) sts remain. Change to 1x1 Rib; work even for 2". BO all sts in pattern.

SLEEVES

Transfer Sleeve sts from waste yarn to needle. With RS facing, using shorter circ needle, rejoin yarn at center underarm. Pick up and knit 0 (3, 5, 9, 10, 13) sts from sts CO for underarm, work to end, pick up and knit 0 (3, 5, 9, 10, 13) sts from sts CO for underarm—82 (90, 98, 106, 114, 120) sts. Join for working in the rnd; pm for beginning of rnd. Continuing in Stripe Pattern, beginning with next rnd after last row worked in Yoke, work even for 1", ending final rnd 2 sts before beginning of next rnd.

Shape Sleeve and Work Stripe Pattern

Note: Each Sleeve shaping rnd begins 2 sts before beginning-of-rnd marker. Change to dpns when necessary for number of sts on needle.

NEXT RND: Decrease 2 sts this rnd, every other rnd 6 (6, 8, 8, 10, 12) times, then every 8 (8, 6, 6, 6, 6) rnds 7 (10, 11, 13, 14, 14) times, working decreases on last 2 sts of rnd and first 2 sts of next rnd as follows: Ssk, sm, k2tog, knit to end—54 (56, 58, 62, 64, 66) sts remain. AT THE SAME TIME, continue working Stripe Pattern as established, working a Jogless Color Change when changing colors, until you have the same number of contrasting color stripes as for Body, then change to 1 strand each of A and B held together. Work even until piece measures 16 (16¼, 16½, 16¾, 17, 17)" from underarm. Change to 1x1 Rib in the Rnd; work even for 2". BO all sts in pattern.

Button Band

With RS facing, using crochet hook and 1 strand each of A and B held together, and beginning at Left Front Neck edge, work Single Crochet (sc) (see Special Techniques, page 156) along Left Front edge, working 3 sts for every 4 rows; work even for 1". Place markers for 7 buttons along Left Front Band, the first ½" from bottom edge, the last ½" below top edge, and the remaining 5 evenly spaced between.

Buttonhole Band

Work as for Button Band, working buttonholes opposite markers when Band measures ½", as follows:

BUTTONHOLE ROW (RS): [Sc to marker, ch2, skip 2 sc] 7 times, sc to end. Complete as for Button Band.

With RS facing, using crochet hook, work 1 row sc around neck edge, working 2 sts for every 3 rows or CO sts.

Sew buttons opposite buttonholes. Weave in all ends. Block as desired.

slate rock cape

For this cape, I chose the sturdy Purl-Twist Fabric stitch from Walker's *A Treasury of Knitting Patterns* (which, because of its smooth density, I find is a perfect choice for outerwear). The no-fuss silhouette, complete with a two-way zipper for added mobility, lends itself to myriad styling options and winter accessories.

STITCH PATTERN

Purl-Twist Fabric

(even number of sts; 4-row repeat)

ROWS 1 AND 3 (RS): Knit.

ROW 2: *P2tog, but do not slip sts from needle, purl first st again, slipping both sts from needle together; repeat from * to end.

ROW 4: P1, *p2tog, but do not slip sts from needle, purl first st again, slipping both sts from needle together; repeat from * to last st, p1.

Repeat Rows 1-4 for Purl-Twist Fabric.

YOKE

Using crochet hook, waste yarn, and Provisional CO (see Special Techniques, page 155), CO 96 (100, 104, 108, 112, 116) sts. Begin Purl-Twist Fabric; work even for 2 rows, placing markers after first 12 (14, 16, 12, 14, 16) sts, then every 12 (12, 12, 14, 14, 14) sts 6 times.

Shape Yoke

NEXT ROW (RS): Increase 14 sts this row, then every other row 9 (11, 13, 15, 17, 19) times, as follows: [Work to marker, M1-b/f] 7 times, work to end—236 (268, 300, 332, 364, 396) sts. *Note: When working shaping, if the st marker is between 2 sts that are to be worked together, slip first st of pair to right-hand needle, remove marker, return slipped st back to left-hand needle, work 2 sts together as instructed, slip last st from right-hand needle back to left-hand needle, replace marker, then slip st back to right-hand needle and continue.*

sizes

X-Small (Small, Medium, Large, 1X-Large, 2X-Large)

finished measurements

53 ½ (59 ¼, 65 ¼, 71, 76 ¾, 82 ¾)" at widest point, including Front Bands and zipper

yarn

Shibui Merino Alpaca (50% baby alpaca / 50% merino wool; 131 yards / 100 grams): 10 (11, 12, 13, 15, 16) hanks Graphite

needles

One 32" (80 cm) long circular (circ) needle size US 8 (5mm)

Change needle size if necessary to obtain gauge.

notions

Crochet hook size US G/6 (4mm); waste yarn; stitch markers; 28 (28, 28, 30, 30, 30)" two-way zipper; sewing needle and matching thread

gauge

22 sts and 24 rows = 4" (10 cm) in Purl-Twist Fabric

15 sts = 4" (10 cm) in Single Crochet (sc)

BODY

Work even until piece measures approximately 12 ½ (13, 13 ½, 14, 14 ½, 15)" from the beginning, ending with Row 4 of Purl-Twist Fabric.

Shape Armhole Openings

NEXT ROW (RS): Work 36 (40, 44, 48, 54, 60) sts, place remaining 200 (228, 256, 284, 310, 336) sts on waste yarn. Working back and forth on remaining 36 (40, 44, 48, 54, 60) sts only, work even in pattern as established for 9", ending with Row 4 of Purl-Twist Fabric. Break yarn, transfer to waste yarn, and set aside.

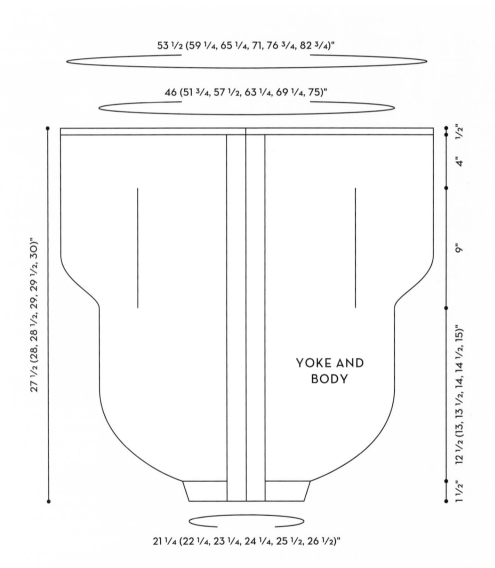

53 ½ (59 ¼, 65 ¼, 71, 76 ¾, 82 ¾)"

46 (51 ¾, 57 ½, 63 ¼, 69 ¼, 75)"

½"

4"

9"

12 ½ (13, 13 ½, 14, 14 ½, 15)"

1 ½"

27 ½ (28, 28 ½, 29, 29 ½, 30)"

YOKE AND BODY

21 ¼ (22 ¼, 23 ¼, 24 ¼, 25 ½, 26 ½)"

Note: Measurements given include crochet trim.

NEXT ROW (RS): Transfer next 164 (188, 212, 236, 256, 276) sts to needle. Rejoin yarn and continuing in pattern as established, work 22 (22, 28, 28, 32, 36) sts, [pm, work 20 (24, 26, 30, 32, 34) sts] 6 times, pm, work 22 (22, 28, 28, 32, 36) sts. Work even for 1 row.

INCREASE ROW (RS): Increase 14 sts this row, then every 4 rows twice, as follows: [Work to marker, M1-b/f, sm] 7 times, work to end—206 (230, 254, 278, 298, 318) sts. Work even until piece measures approximately 9" from beginning of opening, ending with Row 4 of Purl-Twist Fabric. Break yarn, transfer to waste yarn, and set aside.

NEXT ROW (RS): Transfer next 36 (40, 44, 48, 54, 60) sts to needle. Continuing in pattern as established, work even until piece measures approximately 9" from beginning of opening, ending with Row 4 of Purl-Twist Fabric.

NEXT ROW (RS): Transfer held sts back to needle. Continuing in pattern as established across all sts, work even for 4", ending with a WS row—278 (310, 342, 374, 406, 438) sts. BO all sts.

FINISHING

Collar

With RS facing, carefully unravel Provisional CO and place sts on circ needle. Knit 1 row. BO all sts knitwise. With RS facing, using crochet hook, *work 1 row single crochet (sc) (see Special Techniques, page 156), working into each BO st, then work 1 sc decrease row, decreasing 2 sts aligned with each of the 7 Yoke shaping columns; repeat from * once—68 (72, 76, 80, 84, 88) sts remain.

Front Bands

With RS facing, using circ needle, pick up and knit approximately 2 sts in every 3 rows along Front edge. Knit 1 row. BO all sts knitwise. With RS facing, using crochet hook, work 4 rows sc. Sew in zipper. With RS facing, using crochet hook, work 1 row sc around bottom edge.

Armhole Edging

With RS facing, using circ needle, pick up and knit approximately 2 sts in every 3 rows along back edge of armhole (edge furthest from Front Bands). Knit 1 row. BO all sts knitwise. Using crochet hook, work 2 rows sc. With RS facing, using crochet hook, work 1 row sc along front edge of armhole (edge nearest Front Bands). Sew sides of Armhole Edging to top and bottom of Armhole Opening, with back Edging on top of Front Edging, overlapping opening slightly.

Weave in all ends. Block as desired.

nokomis cape

I was excited to find the cable motif I chose for this cape in Walker's *Charted Knitting Designs: A Third Treasury of Knitting Patterns* and immediately recognized it as one she used in a queen-sized orange blanket she showed me when I visited her several years ago in Florida. I remember gasping when I saw it because I understood the hours of work she had put into making it. My reaction made Walker smile, and I named this cape after the town in which our visit took place.

ABBREVIATIONS

3/1 LC-p: Slip 3 sts to cn, hold to front, p1, k3 from cn.

3/1 RC-p: Slip 1 st to cn, hold to back, k3, p1 from cn.

3/3 LC: Slip 3 sts to cn, hold to front, k3, k3 from cn.

3/3 RC: Slip 3 sts to cn, hold to back, k3, k3 from cn.

STITCH PATTERNS

Double X Cable Flat (see Chart, page 41)
(panel of 24 sts; 38-row repeat)

ROW 1 (WS): K2, p6, k8, p6, k2.

ROWS 2 AND 8: P2, 3/3 LC, p8, 3/3 LC, p2.

ROW 3 AND ALL WS ROWS: Knit the knit sts and purl the purl sts as they face you.

ROWS 4 AND 6: P2, k6, p8, k6, p2.

ROW 10: P1, 3/1 RC-p, 3/1 LC-p, p6, 3/1 RC-p, 3/1 LC-p, p1.

ROW 12: 3/1 RC-p, p2, 3/1 LC-p, p4, 3/1 RC-p, p2, 3/1 LC-p.

ROW 14: K3, p4, 3/1 LC-p, p2, 3/1 RC-p, p4, k3.

ROW 16: 3/1 LC-p, p4, 3/1 LC-p, 3/1 RC-p, p4, 3/1 RC-p.

ROW 18: P1, 3/1 LC-p, p4, 3/3 RC, p4, 3/1 RC-p, p1.

ROW 20: P2, 3/1 LC-p, p2, 3/1 RC-p, 3/1 LC-p, p2, 3/1 RC-p, p2.

sizes

X-Small (Small, Medium, Large, 1X-Large, 2X-Large)

finished measurements

46 (52 1/4, 58 1/2, 64 3/4, 71, 77)" at widest point

yarn

Brooklyn Tweed Shelter (100% wool; 140 yards / 50 grams): 7 (8, 9, 10, 11, 12) hanks #05 Long Johns

needles

One 29" (70 cm) long or longer circular (circ) needle size US 8 (5 mm)

Change needle size if necessary to obtain correct gauge.

notions

Crochet hook size US F/5 (3.75 mm); waste yarn; stitch markers; cable needle

gauge

18 sts and 28 rows = 4" (10 cm) in Reverse Stockinette stitch (Rev St st)

ROW 22: P3, 3/1 LC-p, 3/1 RC-p, p2, 3/1 LC-p, 3/1 RC-p, p3.

ROW 24: P4, 3/3 LC, p4, 3/3 LC, p4.

ROW 26: P3, 3/1 RC-p, 3/1 LC-p, p2, 3/1 RC-p, 3/1 LC-p, p3.

ROW 28: P2, 3/1 RC-p, p2, 3/1 LC-p, 3/1 RC-p, p2, 3/1 LC-p, p2.

ROW 30: P1, 3/1 RC-p, p4, 3/3 RC, p4, 3/1 LC-p, p1.

ROW 32: 3/1 RC-p, p4, 3/1 RC-p, 3/1 LC-p, p4, 3/1 LC-p.

ROW 34: K3, p4, 3/1 RC-p, p2, 3/1 LC-p, p4, k3.

ROW 36: 3/1 LC-p, p2, 3/1 RC-p, p4, 3/1 LC-p, p2, 3/1 RC-p.

ROW 38: P1, 3/1 LC-p, 3/1 RC-p, p6, 3/1 LC-p, 3/1 RC-p, p1.

Repeat Rows 1-38 for Double X Cable Flat.

Double X Cable in the Rnd (see Chart, opposite)
(panel of 24 sts; 38-rnd repeat)

RNDS 1 AND 3-7: P2, k6, p8, k6, p2.

RNDS 2 AND 8: P2, 3/3 LC, p8, 3/3 LC, p2.

ROW 9 AND ALL ODD-NUMBERED RNDS: Knit the knit sts and purl the purl sts as they face you.

RND 10: P1, 3/1 RC-p, 3/1 LC-p, p6, 3/1 RC-p, 3/1 LC-p, p1.

RND 12: 3/1 RC-p, p2, 3/1 LC-p, p4, 3/1 RC-p, p2, 3/1 LC-p.

RND 14: K3, p4, 3/1 LC-p, p2, 3/1 RC-p, p4, k3.

RND 16: 3/1 LC-p, p4, 3/1 LC-p, 3/1 RC-p, p4, 3/1 RC-p.

RND 18: P1, 3/1 LC-p, p4, 3/3 RC, p4, 3/1 RC-p, p1.

RND 20: P2, 3/1 LC-p, p2, 3/1 RC-p, 3/1 LC-p, p2, 3/1 RC-p, p2.

RND 22: P3, 3/1 LC-p, 3/1 RC-p, p2, 3/1 LC-p, 3/1 RC-p, p3.

RND 24: P4, 3/3 LC, p4, 3/3 LC, p4.

RND 26: P3, 3/1 RC-p, 3/1 LC-p, p2, 3/1 RC-p, 3/1 LC-p, p3.

RND 28: P2, 3/1 RC-p, p2, 3/1 LC-p, 3/1 RC-p, p2, 3/1 LC-p, p2.

RND 30: P1, 3/1 RC-p, p4, 3/3 RC, p4, 3/1 LC-p, p1.

RND 32: 3/1 RC-p, p4, 3/1 RC-p, 3/1 LC-p, p4, 3/1 LC-p.

RND 34: K3, p4, 3/1 RC-p, p2, 3/1 LC-p, p4, k3.

RND 36: 3/1 LC-p, p2, 3/1 RC-p, p4, 3/1 LC-p, p2, 3/1 RC-p.

RND 38: P1, 3/1 LC-p, 3/1 RC-p, p6, 3/1 LC-p, 3/1 RC-p, p1.

Repeat Rnds 1-38 for Double X Cable Flat.

1x1 Rib
(even number of sts; 1-rnd repeat)

ALL RNDS: *K1, p1; repeat from * to end.

YOKE

CO 1 st for left Front, pm, 15 sts for Left Shoulder/Side, pm, 40 (42, 44, 46, 48, 50) sts for Back, pm, 15 sts for Right Shoulder/Side, pm, and 1 st for right Front—72 (74, 76, 78, 80, 82) sts.

DOUBLE X CABLE

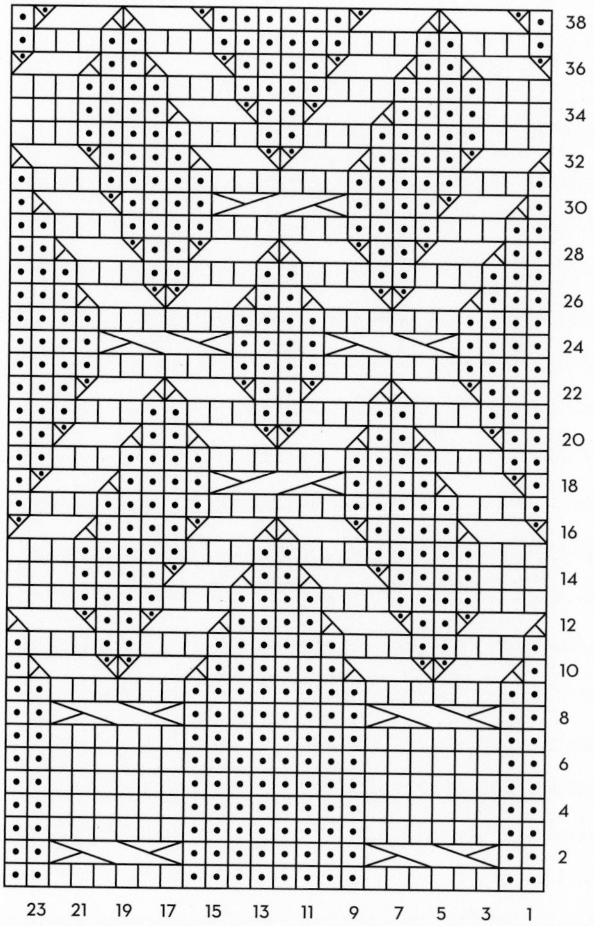
38
36
34
32
30
28
26
24
22
20
18
16
14
12
10
8
6
4
2
23 21 19 17 15 13 11 9 7 5 3 1

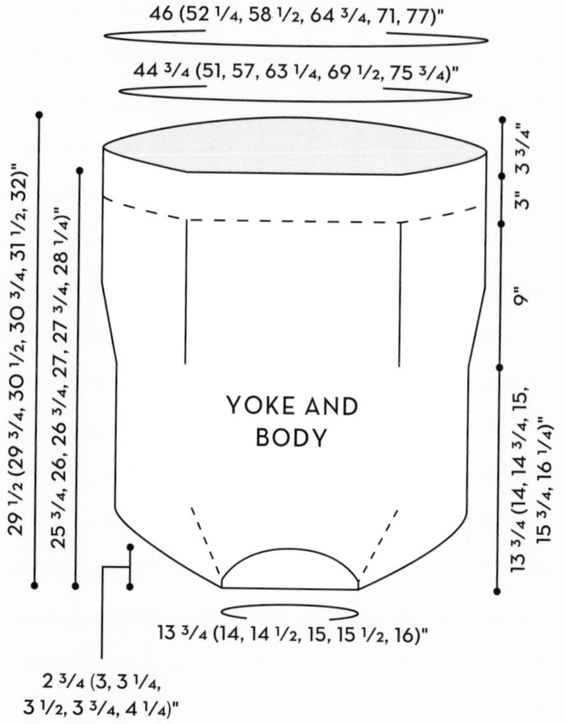
46 (52 1/4, 58 1/2, 64 3/4, 71, 77)"
44 3/4 (51, 57, 63 1/4, 69 1/2, 75 3/4)"
29 1/2 (29 3/4, 30 1/2, 30 3/4, 31 1/2, 32)"
25 3/4, 26, 26 3/4, 27, 27 3/4, 28 1/4)"
3 3/4"
3"
9"
13 3/4 (14, 14 3/4, 15, 15 3/4, 16 1/4)"
YOKE AND BODY
13 3/4 (14, 14 1/2, 15, 15 1/2, 16)"
2 3/4 (3, 3 1/4, 3 1/2, 3 3/4, 4 1/4)"

KEY

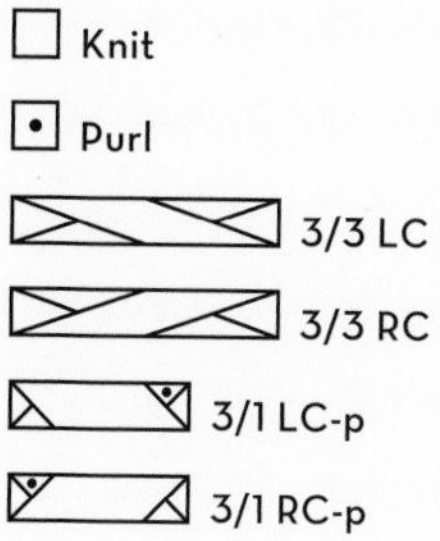
Knit
Purl
3/3 LC
3/3 RC
3/1 LC-p
3/1 RC-p

ROW 1 (WS): Knit to second marker, sm, k8 (9, 10, 11, 12, 13), work Double X Cable Flat over 24 sts, k8 (9, 10, 11, 12, 13), sm, knit to end.

Shape Raglan and Neck

INCREASE ROW 1 (RS): Working Double X Cable Flat as established, and remaining sts in Rev St st, p1-f/b, M1-p-R, sm, p1, M1-p-L, work to 1 st before marker, M1-p-R, p1, sm, M1-p-L, work to marker, M1-p-R, sm, p1, M1-p-L, work to 1 st before marker, M1-p-R, p1, sm, M1-p-L, p1-f/b—82 (84, 86, 88, 90, 92) sts. Work even for 1 row.

INCREASE ROW 2 (RS): Continuing to work in patterns as established, increase 10 sts this row, then every other row 7 (8, 9, 10, 11, 12) times, as follows: P1-f/b, [work to marker, M1-p-R, sm, p1, M1-p-L, purl to 1 st before marker, M1-p-R, p1, sm, M1-p-L] twice, work to last st, p1-f/b—162 (174, 186, 198, 210, 222) sts [19 (21, 23, 25, 27, 29) sts each Front, 33 (35, 37, 39, 41, 43) sts each Side, 58 (62, 66, 70, 74, 78) sts for Back]. Work even for 1 row, making note of last row worked in Double X Cable.

Join Fronts

NEXT ROW (RS): CO 20 sts for Front neck, [work to marker, M1-p-R, sm, p1, M1-p-L, purl to 1 st before marker, M1-p-R, p1, sm, M1-p-L] twice, work to last 2 sts, work Double X Cable in the Rnd, beginning with next rnd after last row worked for Back, over next 24 sts (last 2 sts of row, 20 CO sts, then next 2 sts from Left Front), joining to work in the rnd as you work the cable, work to first marker; this will become new beginning-of-rnd marker—190 (202, 214, 226, 238, 250) sts [60 (64, 68, 72, 76, 80) sts each for Front and Back, 35 (37, 39, 41, 43, 45) sts each Side]. Work even for 1 rnd, working Double X Cable in the Rnd instead of Double X Cable Flat on Back.

Shape Raglan

INCREASE RND: Continuing to work patterns as established, increase 8 sts this rnd, then every 4 (2, 2, 2, 2, 2) rnds 3 (5, 7, 9, 11, 13) times, as follows: [M1-p-R, sm, p1, M1-p-L, work to 1 st before marker, M1-p-R, p1, sm, M1-p-L, work to marker] twice—222 (250, 278, 306, 334, 362) sts [68 (76, 84, 92, 100, 108) sts each for Front and Back, 43 (49, 55, 61, 67, 73) sts each Side].

BODY

Work even until piece measures 11 (11, 11½, 11½, 12, 12)" from Front neck CO, ending wth an even-numbered rnd of Double X Cable in the Rnd. Place next 154 (174, 194, 214, 234, 254) sts on waste yarn, including 2 Back markers; remove first and last markers.

Shape Armhole Openings

NEXT ROW (WS): Working back and forth on remaining 68 (76, 84, 92, 100, 108) sts, work even in patterns as established for 9", ending with a WS row. Break yarn, transfer sts to waste yarn, and set aside.

NEXT ROW (WS): With WS facing, transfer first 154 (174, 194, 214, 234, 254) sts back to needle. Rejoin yarn and work even in patterns as established for 1 row.

INCREASE ROW (RS): Increase 2 sts this row, then every 14 rows twice, as follows: Work to marker, sm, M1-p-L, work to marker, M1-p-R, sm, work to end—160 (180, 200, 220, 240, 260) sts. Work even until piece measures 9" from beginning of opening, ending with a WS row.

Shape Back and Sides

Note: Back and Sides will be shaped using short rows (see Special Techniques, page 153).

SHORT ROW 1 (RS): Work to 16 sts before second marker [9 (13, 17, 21, 25, 29) sts after end of Double X Cable), wrp-t.

SHORT ROW 2 (WS): Work 42 (50, 58, 66, 74, 82) sts, wrp-t.

SHORT ROWS 3–26: Work to wrapped st from row before previous row, hide wrap, work 4 sts, wrp-t.

Rejoin Body

NEXT ROW (RS): With RS facing, pm at left-hand end of circ needle, then transfer remaining sts to left-hand end of circ needle—228 (256, 284, 312, 340, 368) sts. Join for working in the rnd; pm for beginning of rnd. Begin 1x1 Rib; work even for 3", working k2tog at base of each armhole opening on first rnd—226 (254, 282, 310, 338, 366) sts remain. BO all sts in pattern.

FINISHING

With RS facing, using crochet hook, work 1 rnd single crochet (sc) (see Special Techniques, page 156) around neckline.

Armhole Edging

With RS facing, using crochet hook, work 2 rows sc along back edge of armhole (edge furthest from center Front), working 1 sc in 2 of every 3 rows. With RS facing, using crochet hook, work 3 rows sc along front edge of armhole (edge nearest center Front), working 1 sc in 2 of every 3 rows. Sew sides of Armhole Edging to top and bottom of Armhole Opening, with front Edging on top of back edging.

Weave in all ends. Block as desired.

I used short rows to make a hem that falls slightly longer in the back and helps the cape envelop the body like a warm cocoon.

fremont skirt

The simplicity of Walker's skirt template lends itself to infinite design possibilities and inspired me, for this skirt, to incorporate a branch motif from a dress Grace Kelly wore in Alfred Hitchcock's classic film *Rear Window*. I created the motif with simple embroidery stitches and sequins and named the piece after Kelly's character in the film, Lisa Fremont. For an added touch of elegance and finishing, I sewed a piece of black stretch lace to the inside hem edge.

STITCH PATTERN

Linen Stitch

(odd number of sts; 2-rnd repeat)

RND 1: *K1, slip 1 wyif; repeat from * to last st, k1.

RND 2: *Slip 1 wyif, k1; repeat from * to last st, slip 1 wyif.

Repeat Rnds 1 and 2 for Linen Stitch.

SKIRT

CO 151 (171, 191, 211, 231, 251) sts. Join for working in the rnd, being careful not to twist sts; pm for beginning of rnd. Begin Linen Stitch; work even for 1", ending with Rnd 1. Place marker every 30 (34, 38, 42, 46, 50) sts. *Note: The final section will have 31 (35, 39, 43, 47, 51) sts.*

Shape Hip

NEXT RND: Continuing in Linen Stitch, increase 10 sts this rnd, then every 12 rnds 6 (6, 6, 7, 7, 7) times, as follows, working increased sts in Linen Stitch as they become available: [Work to 1 st before marker, k1-f/b/f, sm] 4 times, work to last 2 sts, k1-f/b/f, work 1 st—221 (241, 261, 291, 311, 331) sts. Work even until piece measures 15½ (16, 16½, 17, 17½, 18)", or to desired length from the beginning. BO all sts knitwise.

sizes

X-Small (Small, Medium, Large, X-Large, 2X-Large)

finished measurements

38½ (42, 45½, 50½, 54, 57½)" hip

16 (16½, 17, 17½, 18, 18½)" length

yarn

Rowan Yarns Lima (84% baby alpaca / 8% merino wool / 8% nylon; 109 yards / 50 grams): 7 (8, 9, 10, 11, 12) balls #889 Peru

needles

One 24" (60 cm) long or longer circular (circ) needle size US 9 (5.5mm)

Change needle size if necessary to obtain correct gauge

notions

Crochet hook size US F/5 (3.75 mm); stitch markers; 1 (1, 1, 1¼, 1¼, 1¼) yard(s) thin, round elastic cord; 19¾" x 1 yard package Solvy water-soluble stabilizer; 5 hanks DMC 3 perle cotton embroidery floss in black; sewing needle; 232 black 10 mm sequins; 112 black 12 mm sequins; thin Sharpie marker to match perle cotton embroidery floss; pins or clear packing tape; small cotton towel; spray mist water bottle and water; 1¼ (1¼, 1½, 1½, 1¾, 1¾) yard(s) 1½" stretch black lack trim and matching thread (optional)

gauge

23 sts and 45 rnds = 4" (10 cm) in Linen Stitch

FINISHING

With RS facing, using crochet hook and holding elastic cord parallel to CO edge, work 1 rnd single crochet (sc) (see Special Techniques, page 156) around CO edge and cord. Adjust elastic cord to desired measurement, secure with knot, and weave ends into rnd of sc. Work 1 rnd sc around BO edge.

Weave in all ends. Block as desired.

Embroidery

Enlarge Embroidery Template to desired size. Cut 4 pieces of Solvy and trace template onto each of them with Sharpie. Position Solvy pieces evenly around Skirt, aligning pieces with top edge; secure edges of pieces to Skirt with pins or clear packing tape, being careful not to bunch or wrinkle pieces. Using sewing needle and perle cotton thread, work branches in whipped running stitch (see Special Techniques, page 153) following Template. Attach sequins using perle cotton thread and French knots (see page 154). Spray Solvy pieces using mist water bottle and water to dissolve Solvy, or gently run under tap water and pat out excess water with clean towel. Allow to air dry. Using sewing needle and thread, sew lace to WS of hem.

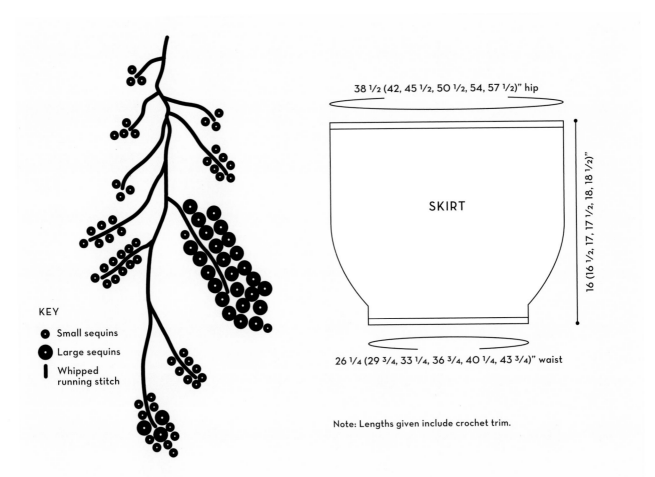

KEY

● Small sequins

● Large sequins

| Whipped running stitch

38 1/2 (42, 45 1/2, 50 1/2, 54, 57 1/2)" hip

SKIRT

16 (16 1/2, 17, 17 1/2, 18, 18 1/2)"

26 1/4 (29 3/4, 33 1/4, 36 3/4, 40 1/4, 43 3/4)" waist

Note: Lengths given include crochet trim.

layered ruffle skirt

Elsebeth Lavold's Silky Wool is a light, lovely yarn that drapes beautifully. For this skirt, I chose to highlight that feature with a series of ruffles worked in various sizes and widths. I worked each ruffle panel separately, and then used a row of single crochet to embed thin elastic cord neatly and invisibly in the top edges, a step that instantly creates multiple evenly placed folds. I then sewed the ruffles to the skirt.

The skirt's fit and length are easy to adjust and customize. You can try the piece on as you go and simply work fewer or more increase rounds, knit to your desired length, and add additional ruffles as needed.

sizes

XX-Small (X-Small, Small, Medium, Large, X-Large)

finished measurements

26 (30, 34, 39 1/2, 44 1/2, 48)" hip

Note: Skirt is intended to fit snugly.

yarn

Elsebeth Lavold Silky Wool (45% wool / 35% silk / 20% nylon; 192 yards / 50 grams): 7 (9, 10, 12, 13, 15) hanks #53 Bronzed Green

needles

One 24" (60 cm) long or longer circular (circ) needle size US 6 (4 mm)

Change needle size if necessary to obtain correct gauge.

notions

Crochet hook size US E/4 (3.5 mm); stitch markers; 2 3/4 (3 1/4, 3 3/4, 4, 4 1/2, 5) yards thin, round elastic cord

gauge

20 sts and 28 rows = 4" (10 cm) in Stockinette st (St st)

SKIRT

CO 110 (130, 150, 168, 192, 210) sts. Join for working in the rnd, being careful not to twist sts; pm for beginning of rnd. Begin St st (knit every rnd); work even until piece measures 4" from the beginning.

Shape Skirt

INCREASE RND 1: *M1, k11 (13, 15, 14, 16, 15); repeat from * to end—120 (140, 160, 180, 204, 224) sts. Work even until piece measures 7 1/2" from the beginning.

INCREASE RND 2: *M1, k12 (14, 16, 10, 12, 14); repeat from * to end—130 (150, 170, 198, 221, 240) sts. Work even until piece measures 14 (14 1/2, 15, 15 1/2, 16, 16 1/2)" from the beginning. ✳ *Customizing Tip:* You may wish to transfer your sts to waste yarn and try the piece on at this point, to make sure the Skirt length is comfortable for you. Work additional rnds if desired. If you work a longer Skirt, you may wish to work one or more of the Ruffles longer, or work an additional Middle Ruffle. ✳ BO all sts.

TOP RUFFLE

CO 99 (117, 135, 151, 173, 189) sts, pm, CO 99 (117, 135, 151, 173, 189) sts—198 (234, 270, 302, 346, 378) sts. Join for working in the rnd, being careful not to twist sts; pm for beginning of rnd.

Shape Ruffle

Note: Ruffle will be shaped using short rows (see Special Techniques, page 153). Work wraps together with wrapped sts as you come to them.

First Half

SHORT ROW 1 (RS): K57 (66, 75, 83, 94, 102), wrp-t.

SHORT ROW 2 (WS): P15, wrp-t.

SHORT ROWS 3 AND 4: Continuing in St st, work to 2 (3, 4, 4, 5, 6) sts past wrapped st of row before previous row, wrp-t.

Repeat Short Rows 3 and 4 until you are 2 (2, 4, 2, 6, 2) sts from each marker.

SHORT ROWS 5 AND 6: Work to 1 st before marker, wrp-t.

Second Half

SHORT ROW 1 (RS): Knit to marker, k57 (66, 75, 83, 94, 102), wrp-t.

Work remaining shaping as for First Half.

Working in the rnd, work even across all sts until piece measures 5" from the beginning, measured at the longest point. BO all sts.

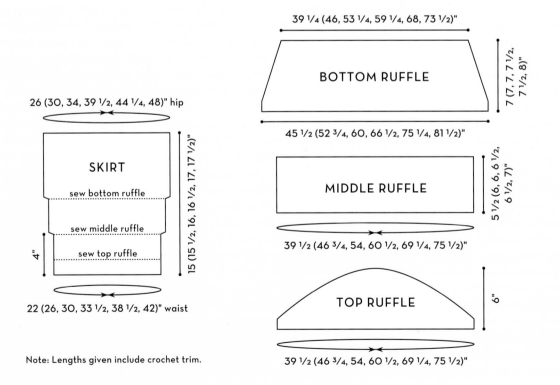

26 (30, 34, 39 1/2, 44 1/4, 48)" hip

SKIRT

sew bottom ruffle

sew middle ruffle

sew top ruffle

4"

15 (15 1/2, 16, 16 1/2, 17, 17 1/2)"

22 (26, 30, 33 1/2, 38 1/2, 42)" waist

Note: Lengths given include crochet trim.

39 1/4 (46, 53 1/4, 59 1/4, 68, 73 1/2)"

BOTTOM RUFFLE

7 (7, 7, 7 1/2, 7 1/2, 8)"

45 1/2 (52 3/4, 60, 66 1/2, 75 1/4, 81 1/2)"

MIDDLE RUFFLE

5 1/2 (6, 6, 6 1/2, 6 1/2, 7)"

39 1/2 (46 3/4, 54, 60 1/2, 69 1/4, 75 1/2)"

TOP RUFFLE

6"

39 1/2 (46 3/4, 54, 60 1/2, 69 1/4, 75 1/2)"

MIDDLE RUFFLE

CO 198 (234, 270, 302, 346, 378) sts. Join for working in the rnd, being careful not to twist sts; pm for beginning of rnd. Begin St st; work even until piece measures 4½ (5, 5, 5½, 5½, 6)" from the beginning. BO all sts.

BOTTOM RUFFLE

CO 228 (264, 300, 332, 376, 408) sts. Do not join. Begin St st; work even for 6 rows.

Shape Ruffle

NEXT ROW (RS): Decrease 1 st each side this row, then every other row 15 (16, 16, 17, 17, 19) times, as follows: K2, ssk, knit to last 4 sts, k2tog, k2—196 (230, 266, 296, 340, 368) sts remain. Work even until piece measures 6 (6, 6, 6½, 6½, 7)" from the beginning, ending with a WS row. BO all sts.

FINISHING

Skirt

With RS of Skirt facing, using crochet hook, and holding elastic cord parallel to CO edge, work 1 rnd single crochet (sc) (see Special Techniques, page 156) around CO edge and cord, working cord into sc. Adjust elastic cord to desired measurements, secure with knot, and weave ends into rnd of sc. With crochet hook, work 3 rnds sc around BO edge.

Top Ruffle

With RS of Top Ruffle facing, using crochet hook and holding elastic cord parallel to CO edge, work 1 rnd around CO edge and cord, working cord into sc. Slide Top Ruffle down over Skirt, 1½" from CO edge of Skirt. Gently pull ends of elastic until Ruffle is same circumference as Skirt; adjust Ruffle so that it is evenly distributed. Secure elastic with knot and weave ends into rnd of sc. Sew to Skirt. With crochet hook, work 3 rnds sc along BO edge.

Middle Ruffle

With RS of Middle Ruffle facing, using crochet hook and holding elastic cord parallel to CO edge, work 1 rnd sc around CO edge and cord, working cord into sc. Slide Middle Ruffle up over Skirt, under Top Ruffle, 2½" below where Top Ruffle is sewn to Skirt. Gather as for Top Ruffle. Sew to Skirt. With crochet hook, work 3 rnds sc along BO edge.

Bottom Ruffle

With RS of Bottom Ruffle facing, using crochet hook and holding elastic cord parallel to CO edge, work 1 rnd sc around CO edge and cord, working cord into sc. With crochet hook and beginning at CO edge, work 1 row sc along first shaping edge, BO edge, then second shaping edge, working sc in every other st along shaped edges, and in every st along BO edge. Work 2 additional rows sc, working 1 sc in each sc. Slide Bottom Ruffle up over Skirt, under Middle Ruffle, 2½ (2¾, 3, 3, 3¼, 3¼)" below where Middle Ruffle is sewn to Skirt. Gather as for Top Ruffle, overlapping edges by 3" at center. Sew to Skirt. Weave in all ends. Block as desired.

knitted pants

Waistlines on pants generally hit higher on the body back in the 1970s when Walker wrote *Knitting from the Top*, and in order to use her pants template to create a modern-day yoga-pant style, I began her template slightly lower. After creating a wide waistband, I immediately worked crotch shaping instead of knitting an additional hip panel or darts as one might for streetwear. What helped most was knowing Walker's template well enough to experiment, and understanding that such exploration is at the heart of top-down knitting and Walker's entire enterprise.

STITCH PATTERNS

2x1 Rib
(multiple of 3 sts; 1-rnd repeat)

ALL RNDS: *K2, p1; repeat from * to end.

1x1 Rib
(multiple of 2 sts; 1-rnd repeat)

ALL RNDS: *K1, p1; repeat from * to end.

WAISTBAND

Using longer circ needle, CO 126 (144, 162, 180, 198, 216) sts. Join for working in rnd, being careful not to twist sts; pm for beginning of rnd. Begin 2x1 Rib; work even until piece measures 4" from beginning, decrease 0 (2, 0, 2, 0, 2) sts on last rnd—126 (142, 162, 178, 198, 214) sts remain.

BODY

NEXT RND: Change to St st; k31 (35, 40, 44, 49, 53), pm, k63 (71, 81, 89, 99, 107), pm, knit to end.

sizes

X-Small (Small, Medium, Large, X-Large, 2X-Large)

finished measurements

38¼ (41, 45¼, 49¾, 53¼, 57)" low hip

yarn

Shelridge Farm Soft Touch W4 (100% wool; 220 yards / 100 grams): 5 (6, 6, 7, 8, 8) hanks Olive

needles

One 24" (60 cm) long or longer circular (circ) needle size US 8 (5 mm)

One 16" (40 cm) long circular needle size US 8 (5 mm)

One set of five double-pointed needles (dpn) size US 8 (5 mm)

Change needle size if necessary to obtain correct gauge.

notions

Crochet hook size US E/4 (3.5 mm); stitch markers; stitch holders or waste yarn; 1 (1, 1, 1¼, 1¼, 1¼) yard(s) thin, round elastic cord

gauge

18 sts and 24 rows = 4" (10 cm) in Stockinette st (St st)

20 sts and 24 rows = 4" (10 cm) in 2x1 Rib

Shape Crotch

INCREASE RND 1: Increase 4 sts this rnd, every 6 rnds 0 (0, 0, 6, 7, 9) times, every 5 rnds 0 (3, 9, 1, 1, 0) time(s), every 4 rnds 3 (4, 0, 1, 1, 0) time(s), every 3 rnds 5 (2, 0, 2, 0, 0) times, then every other rnd 2 (0, 0, 0, 0, 0) times, as follows: [Knit to marker, M1-R, sm, k1, M1-L] twice, knit to end—170 (182, 202, 222, 238, 254) sts. Knit 1 rnd.

INCREASE RND 2: Knit to marker, M1-R, sm, k1, M1-L, knit to next marker; place last 86 (92, 102, 112, 120, 128) sts on st holder or waste yarn for Right Leg, removing marker—86 (92, 102, 112, 120, 128) sts remain.

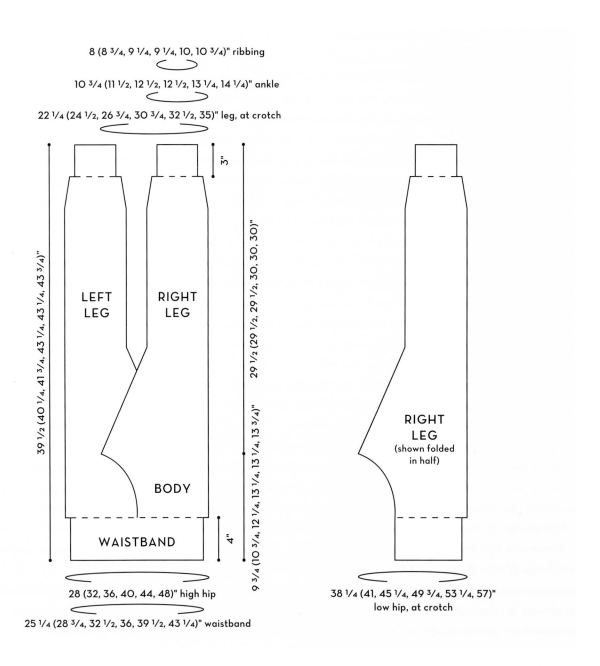

8 (8 3/4, 9 1/4, 9 1/4, 10, 10 3/4)" ribbing

10 3/4 (11 1/2, 12 1/2, 12 1/2, 13 1/4, 14 1/4)" ankle

22 1/4 (24 1/2, 26 3/4, 30 3/4, 32 1/2, 35)" leg, at crotch

3"

LEFT
LEG

RIGHT
LEG

39 1/2 (40 1/4, 41 3/4, 43 1/4, 43 1/4, 43 3/4)"

29 1/2 (29 1/2, 29 1/2, 30, 30, 30)"

9 3/4 (10 3/4, 12 1/4, 13 1/4, 13 1/4, 13 3/4)"

BODY

WAISTBAND

4"

RIGHT
LEG
(shown folded
in half)

28 (32, 36, 40, 44, 48)" high hip

25 1/4 (28 3/4, 32 1/2, 36, 39 1/2, 43 1/4)" waistband

38 1/4 (41, 45 1/4, 49 3/4, 53 1/4, 57)"
low hip, at crotch

LEFT LEG

Note: Change to shorter circ needle for sizes XS, S, and M. ✳ *Customizing Tip: The crotch COs given below will add 3 (4, 4, 5¼, 5¼, 6¾)" to the Leg circumference and crotch length. To ensure a good fit, try the piece on and measure from the bottom of the live sts on the back, through the crotch, to the bottom of the live sts on the front, making sure not to draw your measuring tape too tightly. Multiply this length by the st gauge to determine the number of sts you need to CO for the crotch, rounding to an even number. Adjust the number of CO sts below if necessary, keeping in mind that this will also change the total number of sts for the Leg.* ✳

NEXT RND: CO 7 (9, 9, 13, 13, 15) sts, pm for new beginning of rnd, CO 7 (9, 9, 13, 13, 15), knit to 5 sts before new beginning of rnd marker, knitting into back loop of CO sts if desired to tighten them, pm, k10, pm, knit to new beginning of rnd, removing original beginning of rnd marker at outside of Leg—100 (110, 120, 138, 146, 158) sts.

Shape Thigh

Note: Change to shorter circ, then dpns when necessary for number of sts on needle(s).

NEXT RND: Decrease 2 sts this rnd, then every 4 (4, 3, 3, 2, 2) rnds 15 (16, 17, 22, 24, 28) times, as follows: Knit to marker, sm, ssk, knit to 2 sts before marker, k2tog, sm, knit to end—68 (76, 84, 92, 96, 100) sts remain. Work even until piece measures 23¾ (23, 23¼, 24¼, 24¼, 24¼)" from beginning of Leg, or to 5¾ (6½, 6¼, 5¾, 5¾, 5¾)" from desired length.

Shape Ankle

NEXT RND: Place marker every 17 (19, 21, 23, 24, 25) sts (3 additional markers placed). Decrease 4 sts this rnd, then every 4 (4, 3, 2, 2, 2) rnds 4 (5, 6, 8, 8, 8) times, as follows: [K2tog, knit to marker, sm] 4 times—48 (52, 56, 56, 60, 64) sts remain.

NEXT RND: Change to 1x1 Rib; work even until ribbing measures 3". BO all sts in rib.

RIGHT LEG

Transfer sts from waste yarn to circ needle. Pick up and knit 7 (9, 9, 13, 13, 15) sts from sts CO for Left Leg, pm for new beginning of rnd, pick up and knit 7 (9, 9, 13, 13, 15) sts from sts CO for Left Leg, knit to new beginning of rnd—100 (110, 120, 138, 146, 158) sts. Place marker 5 sts to either side of beginning-of-rnd marker. Complete as for Left Leg.

FINISHING

With RS facing, using crochet hook, and holding elastic cord parallel to CO edge, work 1 rnd single crochet (sc) (see Special Techniques, page 156) around CO edge and cord. Adjust elastic cord to desired measurements, secure with knot, and weave ends into rnd of sc. Close gaps at crotch if necessary. Weave in all ends. Block as desired.

knitted shorts

Who knew a pair of knitted shorts could be so comfortable and flattering? One of the shaping techniques I like most in *Knitting from the Top* is Walker's instruction to shape the crotch before working the legs. Much like the eye-shaped insert found in yoga pants, her crotch shaping largely eliminates unflattering bunching and helps ensure a smooth fit (one you almost have to try to believe)—all seamless and without a bit of sewing.

BODY

Using longer circ needle and A, CO 130 (150, 170, 190, 210, 230) sts. Join for working in the rnd, being careful not to twist sts; pm for beginning of rnd. Work even until piece measures 3 ¼ (3 ½, 3 ½, 3 ¾, 4, 4 ¼)" from the beginning. Change to B. Begin St st; knit 2 rnds.

NEXT RND: [K64 (74, 84, 94, 104, 114), pm, k1] twice.

Shape Crotch

INCREASE RND: Increase 4 sts this rnd, every 3 rnds 1 (1, 1, 2, 2, 2) time(s), every other rnd 3 (3, 3, 4, 4, 4) times, then every rnd 5 (5, 5, 3, 3, 3) times, as follows: [Knit to marker, M1-R, sm, k1, M1-L] twice—170 (190, 210, 230, 250, 270) sts. Knit 1 rnd. Place last 85 (95, 105, 115, 125, 135) sts on waste yarn for Right Leg, removing marker—85 (95, 105, 115, 125, 135) sts remain.

LEFT LEG

✳ *Customizing Tip: The crotch COs given below will add 6" to the Leg circumference and crotch length. To ensure a good fit, try the piece on and measure from the bottom of the live sts on the back, through the crotch, to the bottom of the live sts on the front, making sure not to draw your measuring tape too tightly. Multiply this length by the st gauge to determine the number of sts you need to CO for the crotch, rounding to an even number. Adjust the number of CO sts below if necessary, keeping in mind that this will also change the total number of sts for the Leg.* ✳

sizes
X-Small (Small, Medium, Large, 1X-Large, 2X-Large)

finished measurements
26 (30, 34, 38, 42, 46)" waist

10 ½ (10 ¾, 11, 11 ¾, 12 ¼, 12 ¾)" long

yarn
Sheldridge Farm Soft Touch W4 (100% wool; 220 yards / 100 grams): 1 hank Mulberry (A); 2 (2, 2, 3, 3, 3) hanks Autumn Orange (B)

needles
One 24" (60 cm) long or longer circular (circ) needle size US 7 (4.5 mm)

One 16" (40 cm) long circular needle size US 7 (4.5 mm)

notions
Crochet hook size US E/4 (3.5 mm); stitch markers; waste yarn; 2 yards thin, round elastic cord

gauge
20 sts and 26 rows = 4" (10 cm) in Stockinette st (St st)

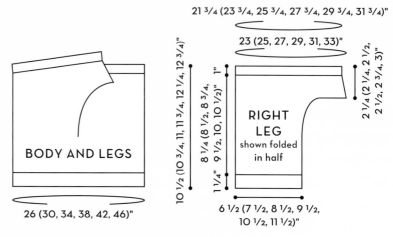

Note: Lengths given include crochet trim.

Using shorter circ needle, CO 15 sts, pm for new beginning of rnd, CO 15 sts, knit to end, knitting into back loop of CO sts if desired to tighten them—115 (125, 135, 145, 155, 165) sts. Work even for 1 rnd.

Shape Thigh

DECREASE RND: Decrease 2 sts this rnd, then every 4 rnds twice, as follows: Knit to marker, sm, ssk, knit to 2 sts before marker, k2tog, sm, knit to end—109 (119, 129, 139, 149, 159) sts remain. ✳ *Customizing Tip: If you prefer a narrower thigh than the pattern calls for, work additional Decrease Rnds, but change to working them every other rnd or every 3 rnds, instead of every 4 rnds, so that you complete them before binding off. Or you may keep the decreases every 4 rnds, and work a longer length before binding off.* ✳ Work even until piece measures 2¼ (2¼, 2½, 2½, 2¾, 3)" from CO sts. BO all sts.

RIGHT LEG

Transfer sts from waste yarn to circ needle. Pick up and knit 15 sts from sts CO for Left Leg, pm for new beginning of rnd, pick up and knit 15 sts from sts CO for Left Leg, knit to new beginning of rnd—115 (125, 135, 145, 155, 165) sts. Complete as for Left Leg.

FINISHING

With RS facing, using crochet hook and A, *work 2 rnds single crochet (sc) (see Special Techniques, page 156) around CO edge. On next rnd, holding elastic cord parallel to CO edge, work 1 rnd sc around CO edge and cord. Repeat from * once. Adjust elastic cords to desired measurements, secure with knots, and weave ends into rnds of sc. With RS facing, using crochet hook and B, work 6 rnds sc around BO edge of each Leg. Close gaps at crotch if necessary.

Weave in all ends. Block as desired.

newest leaves tank

After reading through Walker's sleeveless template, I liked the idea of a go-to piece in a bright, lightweight yarn that could be layered under a blazer or worn on its own. It was springtime when I first started knitting this tank and the leaves on the trees outside of my apartment matched the yarn perfectly. To stabilize the edges of the tank, I worked several rows of crochet, folded it in half, and then sewed it down. One could easily work 3-stitch applied I-cord or a few rows of any non-curling knitted border for a similar effect.

NOTES
※ The Tank is worked in St st, then turned inside-out so that the purl side becomes the RS. If you need to add in a new ball of yarn, be sure to do it on the knit side so that it will not show when the piece is turned inside out.

BACK
Using crochet hook, waste yarn, and Provisional CO (see Special Techniques, page 155), CO 50 (54, 58, 62, 66, 70) sts. Change to working yarn and St st, beginning with a knit row; work even until piece measures 3" from the beginning, ending with a WS row.

Shape Upper Armhole
INCREASE ROW (RS): Increase 1 st each side this row, then every 12 rows once, as follows: K2, M1-R, knit to last 2 sts, M1-L, k2—54 (58, 62, 66, 70, 74) sts. Work even until piece measures 6 (5¾, 5¾, 5¾, 5¾, 5¾)" from the beginning, ending with a WS row.

Shape Armholes
INCREASE ROW (RS): Increase 1 st each side this row, then every other row 9 (10, 11, 12, 13, 14) times, as follows: K2, M1-R, knit to last 2 sts, M1-L, k2—74 (80, 86, 92, 98, 104) sts. Break yarn, transfer sts to waste yarn, and set aside.

sizes
Small (Medium, Large, 1X-Large, 2X-Large, 3X-Large)

finished measurements
32 (36, 40, 44, 48, 52)" bust

yarn
Elsebeth Lavold Silky Wool (45% wool / 35% silk / 20% nylon; 192 yards / 50 grams): 3 (4, 4, 5, 5, 6) hanks #111 Citrine

needles
One 24" (60 cm) long or longer circular (circ) needle size US 6 (4 mm)
Change needle size if necessary to obtain correct gauge

notions
Crochet hook size US D/3 (3.25 mm); waste yarn; stitch markers

gauge
20 sts and 28 rows = 4" (10 cm) in Stockinette stitch (St st)

FRONT

With RS facing, carefully unravel Provisional CO and place sts on circ needle for Front. Mark armhole edge for top of armhole.

NEXT ROW (RS): K6 (7, 8, 10, 11, 12), join a second ball of yarn, BO 38 (40, 42, 42, 44, 46) sts for Back neck, knit to end. Working BOTH SIDES AT THE SAME TIME using separate balls of yarn, work even for 13 rows.

Shape Neck

Note: Neck and Armhole shaping are worked at the same time, and Fronts are joined before neck shaping is complete; please read entire section through before beginning.

INCREASE ROW (RS): Increase 1 st at each neck edge this row, then every 4 rows 7 times, as follows: Right neck edge, knit to last 2 sts, M1-R, k2; left neck edge, k2, M1-L, knit to end—14 (15, 16, 18, 19, 20) sts. Purl 1 row. AT THE SAME TIME, when armholes measure 5¼", work armhole shaping as follows:

Shape Armholes

INCREASE ROW (RS): Continuing with neck shaping as established, increase 1 st each side this row, then every other row 11 (12, 13, 14, 15, 16) times, as follows: K2, M1-R, work to last 2 sts, M1, k2—74 (80, 86, 92, 98, 104) sts. Purl 1 row. AT THE SAME TIME, when neck shaping is complete, join Fronts as follows:

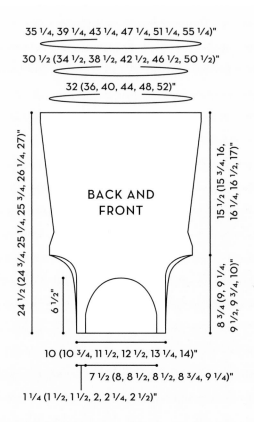

35 ¼, 39 ¼, 43 ¼, 47 ¼, 51 ¼, 55 ¼)"

30 ½ (34 ½, 38 ½, 42 ½, 46 ½, 50 ½)"

32 (36, 40, 44, 48, 52)"

BACK AND FRONT

24 ½ (24 ¾, 25 ¼, 25 ¾, 26 ¼, 27)"

6 ½"

15 ½ (15 ¾, 16, 16 ¼, 16 ½, 17)"

8 ¾ (9, 9 ¼, 9 ½, 9 ¾, 10)"

10 (10 ¾, 11 ½, 12 ½, 13 ¼, 14)"

7 ½ (8, 8 ½, 8 ½, 8 ¾, 9 ¼)"

1 ¼ (1 ½, 1 ½, 2, 2 ¼, 2 ½)"

Join Fronts

NEXT ROW (RS): Continuing with armhole shaping as established, work across right Front sts, CO 22 (24, 26, 26, 28, 30) sts for center neck, work across left Front sts—50 (54, 58, 62, 66, 70) sts. Purl 1 row.

BODY

Join Back to Front

NEXT ROW (RS): Work across Front sts, CO 6 (10, 14, 18, 22, 26) sts for underarm, pm at center of CO sts for side, work across Back sts from waste yarn, CO 6 (10, 14, 18, 22, 26) sts for underarm, pm at center of CO sts for side and beginning of rnd—160 (180, 200, 220, 240, 260) sts. Join for working in the rnd; knit to end. Continuing in St st, work even for 1", ending final rnd 2 sts before beginning of next rnd.

Shape Bust

Note: Each bust shaping rnd begins 2 sts before beginning-of-rnd marker.

DECREASE RND: Decrease 4 sts this rnd, then every 10 (10, 12, 12, 14, 14) rnds once, working decreases on last 2 sts of rnd and first 2 sts of next rnd, as follows: [Ssk, sm, k2tog, knit to 2 sts before marker] twice, knit to end—152 (172, 192, 212, 232, 252) sts remain. Work even until piece measures 8 ½ (8 ¾, 9, 9 ¼, 9 ½, 10)" from underarm, ending last rnd 1 st before beginning-of-rnd marker.

Shape Hip

Note: Each hip shaping rnd begins 1 st before beginning-of-rnd marker.

INCREASE RND: Increase 4 sts this rnd, then every 7 rnds 5 times, as follows: [M1-R, k1, sm, k1, M1-L, knit to 1 st before marker] twice, knit to end—176 (196, 216, 236, 256, 276) sts. Work even until piece measures 15 ½ (15 ¾, 16, 16 ¼, 16 ½, 17)" from underarm. BO all sts.

FINISHING

Turn piece inside out so that purl side is now the RS. With RS facing, using crochet hook, work 2 rnds single crochet (sc) (see Special Techniques, page 156) along bottom edge.

Note: Armhole and neck edging are worked in sc; if you prefer, you may substitute an Applied I-Cord edging instead (see Special Techniques, page 150).

Armhole Edging

With RS facing, using crochet hook and beginning at center underarm, work 4 rnds sc around armhole opening. Fold finished sc in half to WS and sew finished edge to WS, sewing just below top of last sc rnd, and being careful not to let sts show on RS.

Neck Edging

With RS facing, using crochet hook and beginning at left shoulder, work as for armhole edging.

Weave in all ends. Block as desired.

embroidered pullover

This sweater is a variation of Walker's sleeveless template, called the wide-neck blouse. I liked being able to create a neckline that drops in the back, which is made possible by initially working the back as two separate pieces (a left and right side) with provisional cast-ons, and then connecting them after you've cleared the width of your neck. I worked the upper portion of the sweater in Linen Stitch, upon which I embroidered a Mexican-inspired floral motif. After tracing the motif onto dissolvable embroidery stabilizer (a fantastic tool that makes embroidering on knits much easier), I stitched the design with floss and dissolved the stabilizer with water.

STITCH PATTERN

Linen Stitch
(odd number of sts; 2-row repeat)
ROW 1 (RS): K1, *slip 1 wyif, k1; repeat from * to end.
ROW 2: K1, p1, *slip 1 wyib, p1; repeat from * to last st, k1.
Repeat Rows 1 and 2 for Linen Stitch.

BACK

Right Side
Using crochet hook, waste yarn, and Provisional CO (see Special Techniques, page 155), CO 11 (13, 15, 17, 18, 20) sts. Change to shorter circ needle and working yarn. Begin Linen Stitch; work even for 8 rows.

sizes
X-Small (Small, Medium, Large, 1X-Large, 2X-Large)
To fit bust sizes 28–30 (32–34, 36–38, 40–42, 44–46, 48–50)"

finished measurements
38 (42, 45 ¾, 49 ½, 53 ¼, 57 ¼)" bust

yarn
Be Sweet Cotton Candy (100% cotton; 130 yards / 50 grams): 6 (7, 8, 9, 10, 10) hanks #541 Stone

needles
One 32" (80 cm) long or longer circular (circ) needle size US 7 (4.5 mm)
One 16" (40 cm) long circular needle size US 7 (4.5 mm)
Change needle size if necessary to obtain correct gauge.

notions
Crochet hook size US E/4 (3.5 mm); waste yarn; stitch markers; 19 ¾" x 1 yard package Solvy water-soluble stabilizer; 7 hanks DMC 3 perle cotton embroidery floss in white; sewing needle; Gelly Roll Medium Point marker in white; clear packing tape; small cotton towel; spray mist water bottle

gauge
24 sts and 44 rows = 4" (10 cm) in Linen Stitch, after blocking
21 sts and 24 rows = 4" (10 cm) in Stockinette St (St st)

Shape Neck

INCREASE ROW (RS): Increase 2 sts this row, then every 4 rows 9 times as follows, working new sts in pattern as they become available: Work to last st, k1-f/b/f—31 (33, 35, 37, 38, 40) sts. Work even for 1 row.

NEXT ROW (RS): CO 16 (16, 16, 16, 18, 18) sts; do not work across these sts—47 (49, 51, 53, 56, 58) sts. Break yarn and set aside, leaving sts on needle.

Left Side

Using longer circ needle, work as for Right Side to beginning of neck shaping.

Shape Neck

INCREASE ROW (RS): Increase 2 sts this row, then every 4 rows 9 times, as follows, working new sts in pattern as they become available: Work to last st, k1-f/b/f—31 (33, 35, 37, 38, 40) sts. Work even for 1 row.

Join Sides

NEXT ROW (RS): Continuing in Linen Stitch, work to last st of Left Side, k2tog (last st of Left Side together with first st of Right Side), work in Linen Stitch to end, beginning with slip 1 wyif—77 (81, 85, 89, 93, 97) sts. Work even until piece measures 8 (8, 7¾, 7¾, 8, 8)" from the beginning, ending with a WS row.

NEXT ROW (RS): Change to St st. K10, *M1, k14 (15, 16, 17, 18, 19); repeat from * to last 11 sts, M1, knit to end—82 (86, 90, 94, 98, 102) sts. Purl 1 row.

Shape Armholes

INCREASE ROW (RS): Increase 1 st each side this row, then every other row 4 (6, 8, 10, 12, 14) times, as follows: K2, M1-R, knit to last 2 sts, M1-L, k2—92 (100, 108, 116, 124, 132) sts. Purl 1 row. Break yarn, transfer sts to waste yarn, and set aside.

FRONT

With RS facing, carefully unravel Provisional COs and place Right and Left Side sts on longer circ needle. Mark armhole edge for top of armhole. Working BOTH SIDES AT THE SAME TIME using separate balls of yarn, work as for Back to end of neck increases—31 (33, 35, 37, 38, 40) sts each Side. Work even for 1 row.

Shape Neck Slit

NEXT ROW (RS): Continuing in Linen Stitch, on Right Side, work to end, CO 8 (8, 8, 8, 9, 9) sts; on Left Side, CO 8 (8, 8, 8, 9, 9) sts, work to end—39 (41, 43, 45, 47, 49) sts each side. Work even until piece measures 3¼" from beginning of neck slit, ending with a WS row. Break yarn for Left Side.

Join Sides

NEXT ROW (RS): Continuing in Linen Stitch, work to last st of Right Side, k2tog (last st of Right Side together with first st of Left Side), work in Linen Stitch to end, beginning with slip 1 wyif—77 (81, 85, 89, 93, 97) sts. Work even if necessary until piece measures same as for Back from marker to beginning of St st, ending with a WS row.

NEXT ROW (RS): Change to St st. K10, *M1, k14 (15, 16, 17, 18, 19); repeat from * to last 11 sts, M1, knit to end—82 (86, 90, 94, 98, 102) sts. Purl 1 row. Shape armholes as for Back—92 (100, 108, 116, 124, 132) sts. Purl 1 row. Do not break yarn; leave sts on needle.

BODY

Join Back and Front

With RS of Back and Front facing, transfer Back sts to left-hand end of circ needle. Knit across Front sts, CO 8 (10, 12, 14, 16, 18) sts for underarm, knit across Back sts, CO 8 (10, 12, 14, 16, 18) sts for underarm—200 (220, 240, 260, 280, 300) sts. Join for working in the rnd; pm for beginning of rnd. Continuing in St st, work even until piece measures 9 1/4 (9 1/2, 9 3/4, 9 1/2, 9 1/2, 9 1/4)" from underarm.

Shape Hips

DECREASE RND 1: *K18 (20, 22, 24, 26, 28), k2tog; repeat from * to end—190 (210, 230, 250, 270, 290) sts remain. Knit 6 rnds.

DECREASE RND 2: *K17 (19, 21, 23, 25, 27), k2tog; repeat from * to end—180 (200, 220, 240, 260, 280) sts remain. Knit 6 rnds.

DECREASE RND 3: *K16 (18, 20, 22, 24, 26), k2tog; repeat from * to end—170 (190, 210, 230, 250, 270) sts remain. Work even until piece measures 13 1/4 (13 1/2, 13 3/4, 13 3/4, 13 1/2, 13 1/4)" from underarm. BO all sts.

SLEEVES

With RS facing, using shorter circ needle and beginning at center of underarm, pick up and knit 90 (96, 102, 108, 114, 120) sts evenly around armhole. Join for working in the rnd; pm for beginning of rnd.

Shape Cap

Note: Cap is shaped using short rows (see Special Techniques, page 153).

SHORT ROW 1 (RS): K60 (64, 68, 72, 76, 80), wrp-t.

SHORT ROW 2: P30 (32, 34, 36, 38, 40), wrp-t.

SHORT ROWS 3–22 (24, 26, 28, 30, 32): Work to wrapped st from row before previous row, hide wrap, wrp-t—20 (21, 22, 23, 24, 25) sts remain unworked on either side of underarm marker. Work even for 2 (2, 2, 4, 4, 4) rnds, hiding remaining wraps as you come to them on first rnd. BO all sts.

FINISHING

With RS facing, using crochet hook and working yarn, work 3 rnds single crochet (sc) (see Special Techniques, page 156) along bottom edge, and 1 rnd sc along Sleeve edges. With RS facing, using crochet hook and embroidery floss, work 1 rnd sc in every other st around neckline, bottom edge, and Sleeves.

With RS facing, using crochet hook and embroidery floss, work 1 row sc in every other st for crochet "seam" across last row of Linen Stitch at beginning of armhole shaping on Front and Back.

Provisional cast-ons enable a flattering scoop in the back of this sweater.

Weave in all ends. Block as desired.

Embroidery

Photocopy Embroidery Template, enlarging 129%, or to desired size.
Cut 2 pieces of Solvy and trace 1 Template onto each piece with gel pen.
Position pieces evenly on either side of Front slit (see photos), and, working
one at a time, secure edges of Solvy to sweater with clear packing tape or
pins, being careful not to bunch or wrinkle Solvy. Using sewing needle and
embroidery floss, and following Templates, work stems with Backstitch
(see Special Techniques, page 150), flowers and petals with Satin stitch
(see Special Techniques, page 153), and berries with French Knots (see Special
Techniques, page 154). *Note: When working Satin stitch, work sts widthwise
across the petals and flowers, not lengthwise.* Spray Solvy pieces using mist bottle
and water to dissolve Solvy, or gently run under tap water and pat out excess
water with a clean towel. Allow to air dry.

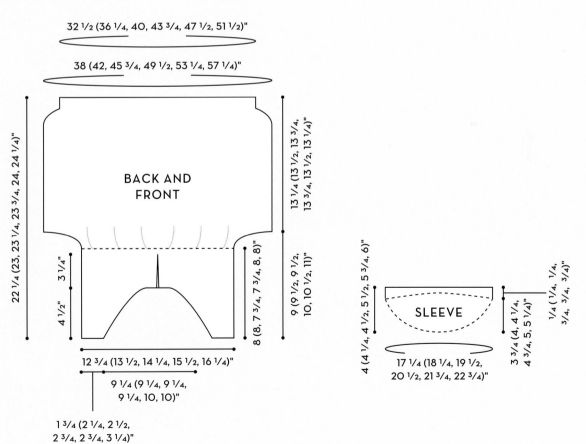

32 1/2 (36 1/4, 40, 43 3/4, 47 1/2, 51 1/2)"

38 (42, 45 3/4, 49 1/2, 53 1/4, 57 1/4)"

BACK AND FRONT

13 1/4 (13 1/2, 13 3/4, 13 3/4, 13 1/2, 13 1/4)"

22 1/4 (23, 23 1/4, 23 3/4, 24, 24 1/4)"

3 1/4"

4 1/2"

9 (9 1/2, 9 1/2, 10, 10 1/2, 11)"

8 (8, 7 3/4, 7 3/4, 8, 8)"

12 3/4 (13 1/2, 14 1/4, 15 1/2, 16 1/4)"

9 1/4 (9 1/4, 9 1/4, 9 1/4, 10, 10)"

1 3/4 (2 1/4, 2 1/2, 2 3/4, 2 3/4, 3 1/4)"

SLEEVE

4 (4 1/4, 4 1/2, 5 1/2, 5 3/4, 6)"

3 3/4 (4, 4 1/4, 4 3/4, 5, 5 1/4)"

1/4 (1 1/4, 1/4, 3/4, 3/4, 3/4)"

17 1/4 (18 1/4, 19 1/2, 20 1/2, 21 3/4, 22 3/4)"

oak dress

The wonderfully tailored look you can achieve with Walker's set-in sleeve template inspired me to make several dresses for my first book, *Modern Top-Down Knitting*. And the kind letters I continue to receive from knitters all over the world who have made them encouraged me to design another for this book. The lovely drape of Elsebeth Lavold's Silky Wool helped me create a lightweight, flattering dress that moves with both comfort and grace.

sizes
X-Small (Small, Medium, Large, 1X-Large, 2X-Large)

finished measurements
32 ½ (36 ½, 40 ½, 44 ½, 48 ½, 52 ½)" bust

yarn
Elsebeth Lavold Silky Wool (45% wool / 35% silk / 20% nylon; 192 yards / 50 grams): 7 (8, 9, 10, 11, 12) hanks Dark Oak #86

needles
One 29" (70 cm) long circular (circ) needle size US 6 (4 mm)

One 16" (40 cm) long circular needle size US 6 (4 mm)

Change needle size if necessary to obtain correct gauge

notions
Crochet hook size US D/3 (3.25 mm); crochet hook size US E/4 (3.5 mm); waste yarn; stitch markers; 3 (4, 5, 5, 6, 7) ⅜" buttons; 1 yard thin, round elastic cord

gauge
20 sts and 28 rows = 4" in Stockinette stitch (St st)

STITCH PATTERNS

Seed Stitch
(odd number of sts; 1-row/rnd repeat)

ROW/RND 1: P1, *k1, p1; repeat from * to end.

ROW/RND 2: Knit the purl sts and purl the knit sts as they face you.

Repeat Row/Rnd 2 for Seed Stitch.

BACK

Using larger crochet hook, waste yarn, and Provisional CO (see Special Techniques, page 155), CO 71 (75, 79, 83, 87, 91) sts. Change to shorter circ needle and working yarn. Begin St st; work even until piece measures 7 ¼ (7, 6 ½, 6 ¼, 6 ¼, 6 ¼)" from the beginning, ending with a WS row.

Shape Armholes
INCREASE ROW (RS): Increase 1 st each side this row, then every other row 1 (4, 6, 8, 10, 12) time(s), as follows: K2, M1-R, knit to last 2 sts, M1-L, k2—75 (85, 93, 101, 109, 117) sts. Purl 1 row. Break yarn and set aside, leaving sts on needle.

FRONT

With RS facing, carefully unravel Provisional CO and place sts on longer circ needle. Mark armhole edge for top of armhole.

NEXT ROW (RS): K9 (10, 12, 13, 14, 16), join a second ball of yarn, BO 53 (55, 55, 57, 59, 59) sts for Back neck, knit to end—9 (10, 12, 13, 14, 16) sts remain each side for shoulders. Working BOTH SIDES AT THE SAME TIME using separate balls of yarn, purl 1 row.

Shape Neck and Armholes

Note: Neck and armhole shaping are worked at the same time; neck shaping will not be completed until after Back and Fronts are joined. Please read entire section through before beginning.

INCREASE ROW (RS): Increase 1 st each neck edge this row, every other row 15 (16, 16, 17, 18, 18) times, then every four rows 12 times, as follows: On right neck edge, work to last 2 sts, M1-L, k2; on left neck edge, k2, M1-R, knit to end. AT THE SAME TIME, when armholes measure same as for Back from marker to beginning of armhole shaping, shape armholes as for Back. *Note: When armhole shaping is complete, there are 32 (38, 42, 46, 50, 55) sts for each Front, if row gauge was matched exactly. You may have a few sts more or less at this point due to differences in row gauge and measuring.*

BODY

Join Back and Fronts

NEXT ROW (RS): Continuing with neck shaping as established, work across Left Front sts, CO 0 (0, 2, 4, 6, 8) sts for underarm, pm in center of CO sts to mark side (between Front and Back for sizes XS and S), work across Back sts, CO 0 (0, 2, 4, 6, 8) sts for underarm, pm in center of CO sts to mark side, then work across Right Front sts. Purl 1 row, ending 2 sts before beginning-of-rnd marker.

Note: Each waist shaping rnd begins 2 sts before beginning-of-rnd marker.

SHAPE WAIST (RS): Continuing with neck shaping, decrease 4 sts this row, every 8 (8, 8, 8, 10, 10) rows 1 (1, 0, 0, 3, 3) time(s), then every 10 (10, 10, 10, 12, 12) rows 3 (3, 4, 4, 1, 1) time(s), working decreases on last 2 sts of rnd and first 2 sts of next rnd as follows: [ssk, sm, k2tog, knit to 2 sts before marker] twice, work to end—133 (153, 173, 193, 213, 233) sts when all shaping is complete. Leave sts on needle.

Neckband

With RS facing, using shorter circ needle and beginning at lower Right Front edge, pick up and knit 70 (72, 72, 74, 76, 76) sts to right shoulder, 53 (55, 55, 57, 59, 59) sts across Back neck, then 70 (72, 72, 74, 76, 76) sts to lower Left Front edge—193 (199, 199, 205, 211, 211) sts. Begin Seed Stitch; work even for 6 rows. BO all sts purlwise.

SKIRT

Rejoin yarn to Left Front; pick up and knit 5 sts from side edge of Neckband, knit to end, pick up and knit 5 sts from side edge of Neckband—143 (163,

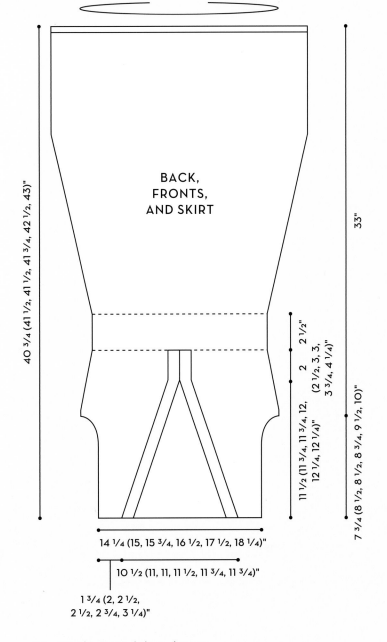

40 (44, 48, 52, 56, 60)" hips
28 1/2 (32 1/2, 36 1/2, 40 1/2, 44 1/2, 48 1/2)" waist
32 1/2 (36 1/2, 40 1/2, 44 1/2, 48 1/2, 52 1/2)" bust
BACK, FRONTS, AND SKIRT
40 3/4 (41 1/2, 41 1/2, 41 3/4, 42 1/2, 43)"
33"
2 1/2"
2 (2 1/2, 3, 3, 3 3/4, 4 1/4)"
11 1/2 (11 3/4, 11 3/4, 12, 12 1/4, 12 1/4)"
7 3/4 (8 1/2, 8 1/2, 8 3/4, 9 1/2, 10)"
14 1/4 (15, 15 3/4, 16 1/2, 17 1/2, 18 1/4)"
10 1/2 (11, 11, 11 1/2, 11 3/4, 11 3/4)"
1 3/4 (2, 2 1/2, 2 1/2, 2 3/4, 3 1/4)"
SLEEVE
18 (18 1/4, 18 3/4, 19 1/4, 20, 20 1/4)"
12 (12, 12 1/4, 12 1/2, 12 3/4, 12 3/4)"
6 (6 1/4, 6 1/2, 6 3/4, 7 1/4, 7 1/2)"
14 1/2 (15 1/2, 16 3/4, 18, 19 1/2, 21 1/4)"

Note: Lengths given include crochet trim.

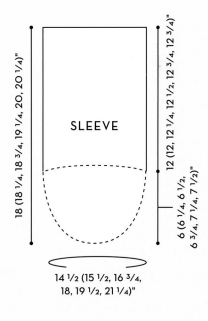

183, 203, 223, 243) sts. Join for working in the rnd; pm for beginning of rnd. Begin Seed Stitch; work even for 2½". Change to St st; work even for 3 rnds, increasing 2 sts evenly on first rnd, and placing markers every 29 (33, 37, 41, 45, 49) sts on last rnd—145 (165, 185, 205, 225, 245) sts.

Shape Skirt

INCREASE RND: Increase 5 sts this rnd, then every 10 rnds 10 times, as follows: *M1, knit to next marker, sm; repeat from * to end—200 (220, 240, 260, 280, 300) sts. Work even until piece measures 32½" from underarm, or to desired length. BO all sts.

SLEEVES

With RS facing, using shorter circ needle and beginning at center of underarm, pick up and knit 72 (78, 84, 90, 98, 106) sts evenly around armhole. Join for working in the rnd; pm for beginning of rnd.

Shape Cap

Note: Cap is shaped using short rows (see Special Techniques, page 153).

SHORT ROW 1 (RS): K49 (52, 57, 60, 66, 72), wrp-t.

SHORT ROW 2: P26 (26, 30, 30, 34, 38), wrp-t.

SHORT ROWS 3–42 (44, 46, 48, 50, 52): Work to wrapped st from row before previous row, hide wrap, wrp-t—3 (5, 5, 7, 8, 9) sts remain unworked on either side of underarm marker. Work even, hiding remaining wrap as you come to it, until piece measures 12 (12, 12¼, 12½, 12¾, 12¾)" from underarm. BO all sts.

FINISHING

Using larger crochet hook, work 4 rnds single crochet (sc) (see Special Techniques, page 156) along bottom edge.

Button Loops

With RS facing, using smaller crochet hook, join yarn at bottom corner of Right Front Neckband, slip st 2, [ch 10, slip st in first 4 sts of ch 10 (button loop made)], *slip st 4, make button loop; repeat from * 1 (2, 3, 3, 4, 5) time(s), slip st to end. Sew buttons opposite Button loops.

Sleeve Edging

With RS facing, using larger crochet hook and holding elastic cord parallel to edge, work 1 rnd sc around Sleeve edge and cord. Adjust elastic cord to desired measurements, tie in knot to secure, and weave ends into rnd of sc.

Weave in all ends. Block as desired.

maple shade coat

This coat was conceived out of a practical concern: the common experience of feeling cold in an overly air-conditioned office building. I loved the idea of making a warm coatlike sweater that would go with everything and feel like a hug when you put it on. I'm pleased to say that this piece fits the bill. Walker's intricate Woodgrain II stitch pattern (from *A Third Treasury of Knitting Patterns*) provides an added sense of home for me, since it reminds me of the gnarled roots of a maple tree in the front yard of the house I grew up in.

ABBREVIATIONS

3/3 LC: Slip 3 sts to cn and hold to front, k3, k3 from cn.

3/3 RC: Slip 3 sts to cn and hold to back, k3, k3 from cn.

1/2 LC-p: Slip 2 sts to cn and hold to front, k1, p2 from cn.

1/2 RC-p: Slip 2 sts to cn and hold to back, k1, p2 from cn.

STITCH PATTERNS

Woodgrain II (see Chart, page 82)
(multiple of 14 sts; 36-row repeat)

ROW 1 (RS): P3, *p1, k6, p7; repeat from * to last 11 sts, p1, k6, p4.

ROW 2 AND ALL WS ROWS: Knit the knit sts and purl the purl sts as they face you.

ROW 3: P3, *p1, 3/3 RC, p7; repeat from * to last 11 sts, p1, 3/3 RC, p4.

ROW 5: Repeat Row 2.

ROW 7: P2, *1/2 RC-p, k4, 1/2 LC-p, p4; repeat from * to last 12 sts, 1/2 RC-p, k4, 1/2 LC-p, p2.

ROW 9: 1/2 RC-p, *p2, k4, p2, 1/2 LC-p, 1/2 RC-p; repeat from * to last 11 sts, p2, k4, p2, 1/2 LC-p.

sizes
X-Small (Small, Medium, Large, 1X-Large, 2X-Large)

finished measurements
33 (37, 41, 45, 49, 53)" bust, snapped

yarn
Blue Sky Alpacas Worsted Hand Dyes (50% royal alpaca / 50% merino wool; 100 yards / 100 grams): 12 (13, 14, 16, 17, 18) hanks #2015 Putty

needles
One 29" (70 cm) long or longer circular (circ) needle size US 8 (5 mm)

One 16" (40 cm) long circular needle size US 8 (5 mm)

Change needle size if necessary to obtain correct gauge.

notions
Crochet hook size US G/6 (4.25 mm); waste yarn; cable needle; stitch markers; 2 yards 1" wide coordinating cotton twill tape; 9 size 10 sew-on snaps; sewing needle and matching thread

gauge
16 sts and 23 rows = 4" (10 cm) in Stockinette stitch (St st)

18 1/2 sts and 22 rows = 4" (10 cm) in Woodgrain II

ROW 11: K1, p2, *1/2 RC-p, k2, 1/2 LC-p, p2, k2, p2; repeat from * to last 11 sts, 1/2 RC-p, k2, 1/2 LC-p, p2, k1.

ROW 13: K1, *1/2 RC-p, p2, k2, p2, 1/2 LC-p, k2; repeat from * to last 13 sts, 1/2 RC-p, p2, p2, 1/2 LC-p, k1.

ROW 15: K2, p1, *p1, 1/2 RC-p, 1/2 LC-p, p2, k4, p1; repeat from * to last 11 sts, p1, 1/2 RC-p, 1/2 LC-p, p2, k2.

ROW 17: K2, *1/2 RC-p, p4, 1/2 LC-p, k4; repeat from * to last 12 sts, 1/2 RC-p, p4, 1/2 LC-p, k2.

ROW 19: Repeat Row 2.

ROW 21: K3, *p8, 3/3 LC; repeat from * to last 11 sts, p8, k3.

ROW 23: Repeat Row 2.

ROW 25: K2, *1/2 LC-p, p4, 1/2 RC-p, k4; repeat from * to last 12 sts, 1/2 LC-p, p4, 1/2 RC-p, k2.

ROW 27: K2, p1, *p1, 1/2 LC-p, 1/2 RC-p, p2, k4, p1; repeat from * to last 11 sts, p1, 1/2 LC-p, 1/2 RC-p, p2, k2.

ROW 29: K1, 1/2 LC-p, *p2, k2, p2, 1/2 RC-p, k2, 1/2 LC-p; repeat from * to last 10 sts, p2, k2, p2, 1/2 RC-p, k1.

ROW 31: K1, p2, *1/2 LC-p, k2, 1/2 RC-p, p2, k2, p2; repeat from * to last 11 sts, 1/2 LC-p, k2, 1/2 RC-p, p2, k1.

ROW 33: 1/2 LC-p, *p2, k4, p2, 1/2 RC-p, 1/2 LC-p; repeat from * to last 11 sts, p2, k4, p2, 1/2 RC-p.

ROW 35: P2, *1/2 LC-p, k4, 1/2 RC-p, p4; repeat from * to last 12 sts, 1/2 LC-p, k4, 1/2 RC-p, p2.

ROW 36: Repeat Row 2.

Repeat Rows 1–36 for Woodgrain II.

Right Woodgrain II (see Chart, page 82)
(panel of 30 sts; 18 rows)

ROW 1 (RS): P1, k2, 1/2 LC-p, p2, k2, p2, 1/2 RC-p, k2, 1/2 LC-p, p2, k1, p2, k2, p2, k1.

ROW 2 AND ALL WS ROWS: Knit the knit sts and purl the purl sts as they face you.

ROW 3: P1, k2, p2, 1/2 LC-p, k2, 1/2 RC-p, p2, k2, p2, 1/2 LC-p, k1, p2, k2, p2, k1.

ROW 5: P2, 1/2 LC-p, p2, k4, p2, 1/2 RC-p, 1/2 LC-p, p2, k2, p2, k2, p2, k1.

ROW 7: P4, 1/2 LC-p, k4, 1/2 RC-p, p4, 1/2 LC-p, [k2, p2] twice, k1.

ROW 9: P6, k6, p8, k3, p2, k2, p2, k1.

ROW 11: P6, 3/3 LC, p8, k3, p2, k2, p2, k1.

ROW 13: P6, k6, p8, k3, p2, k2, p2, k1.

ROW 15: P4, 1/2 RC-p, k4, 1/2 LC-p, p4, 1/2 RC-p, k2, p2, k2, p2, k1.

ROW 17: P2, 1/2 RC-p, p2, k4, p2, 1/2 LC-p, 1/2 RC-p, p2, k2, p2, k2, p2, k1.

ROW 18: Repeat Row 2.

Left Woodgrain II (see Chart, page 82)
(panel of 30 sts; 18 rows)

ROW 1 (RS): K1, p2, k2, p2, k1, p2, 1/2 RC-p, k2, 1/2 LC-p, p2, k2, p2, 1/2 RC-p, k2, p1.

ROW 2 AND ALL WS ROWS: Knit the knit sts and purl the purl sts as they face you.

ROW 3: K1, p2, k2, p2, k1, 1/2 RC-p, p2, k2, p2, 1/2 LC-p, k2, 1/2 RC-p, p2, k2, p1.

ROW 5: K1, p2, [k2, p2] twice, 1/2 RC-p, 1/2 LC-p, p2, k4, p2, 1/2 RC-p, p2.

ROW 7: K2, [p2, k2] twice, p2, k2, 1/2 RC-p, p4, 1/2 LC-p, k4, 1/2 RC-p, p4.

ROW 9: Repeat Row 2.

ROW 11: K1, p2, k2, p2, k3, p8, 3/3 LC, p6.

ROW 13: Repeat Row 2.

ROW 15: K1, [p2, k2] twice, 1/2 LC-p, p4, 1/2 RC-p, k4, 1/2 LC-p, p4.

ROW 17: K1, p2, [k2, p2] twice, 1/2 LC-p, 1/2 RC-p, p2, k4, p2, 1/2 LC-p, p2.

ROW 18: Repeat Row 2.

2x2 Rib for Body
(multiple of 4 sts; 1-row repeat)

ROW 1 (WS): P3, *k2, p2; repeat from * to last st, p1.

ROW 2: Knit the knit sts and purl the purl sts as they face you.

Repeat Row 2 for 2x2 Rib for Body.

2x2 Rib for Sleeves
(multiple of 4 sts; 1-rnd repeat)

ALL RNDS: P1, *k2, p2; repeat from * to last 3 sts, k2, p1.

BACK

Using crochet hook, waste yarn, and Provisional CO (see Special Techniques, page 155), CO 60 (64, 70, 74, 78, 80) sts. Change to working yarn and longer circ needle.

NEXT ROW (RS): P0 (2, 0, 0, 2, 2), k2 (2, 0, 2, 2, 3), work Woodgrain II (from text or Chart) over next 56 (56, 70, 70, 70, 70) sts, k2 (2, 0, 2, 2, 3), p0 (2, 0, 0, 2, 2). Continuing to work center sts in Woodgrain II, and sts before and after Woodgrain II (if applicable) in either knit or purl as established, work Rows 2-36 of Woodgrain II once, then Rows 1-6 once.

Shape Armholes

NEXT ROW (RS): Change to St st. Increase 1 st each side this row, then every other row 0 (2, 3, 3, 4, 6) times, as follows: K2, M1-R, knit to last 2 sts, M1-L, k2—62 (70, 78, 82, 88, 94) sts. Break yarn, transfer sts to waste yarn, and set aside.

FRONTS

With RS facing, carefully unravel Provisional CO and place sts on longer circ needle for Right Front. Mark armhole edge for top of armhole.

Begin Pattern and Shape Neck

Note: Pattern and neck shaping will be worked at the same time; please read entire section through before beginning.

NEXT ROW (WS): K0 (2, 0, 0, 2, 2), p2 (2, 0, 2, 2, 3), work Woodgrain II across 12 (11, 17, 16, 15, 15) sts, beginning with st 28 of Row 4 of Chart, join a second ball of yarn, BO 32 (34, 36, 38, 40, 40) sts for Back neck, work Woodgrain II to end, beginning with st 12 (11, 17, 16, 15, 15) of Row 4 of Chart, p2 (2, 0, 2, 2, 3), k0 (2, 0, 0, 2, 2). Working BOTH SIDES AT THE SAME TIME using separate balls of yarn, and continuing to work patterns as established, work Rows 5–36 of Chart once, then Rows 1–6. AT THE SAME TIME, beginning with Row 5 of Woodgrain II, begin neck shaping.

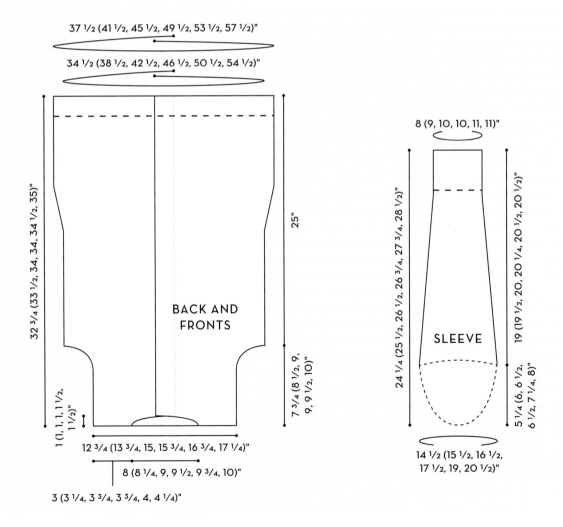

37 1/2 (41 1/2, 45 1/2, 49 1/2, 53 1/2, 57 1/2)"

34 1/2 (38 1/2, 42 1/2, 46 1/2, 50 1/2, 54 1/2)"

32 3/4 (33 1/2, 34, 34, 34 1/2, 35)"

25"

BACK AND FRONTS

7 3/4 (8 1/2, 9, 9, 9 1/2, 10)"

1 (1, 1, 1, 1 1/2, 1 1/2)"

12 3/4 (13 3/4, 15, 15 3/4, 16 3/4, 17 1/4)"

8 (8 1/4, 9, 9 1/2, 9 3/4, 10)"

3 (3 1/4, 3 3/4, 3 3/4, 4, 4 1/4)"

8 (9, 10, 10, 11, 11)"

24 1/4 (25 1/2, 26 1/2, 26 3/4, 27 3/4, 28 1/2)"

19 (19 1/2, 20, 20 1/4, 20 1/2, 20 1/2)"

SLEEVE

5 1/4 (6, 6 1/2, 6 1/2, 7 1/4, 8)"

14 1/2 (15 1/2, 16 1/2, 17 1/2, 19, 20 1/2)"

NEXT ROW (RS): Increase 1 st at each neck edge this row, then every other row 2 (2, 2, 2, 3, 3) times, working increased sts in Woodgrain II as they become available, as follows: For Right Front, work to last st, p1-f/b; for Left Front, p1-f/b, work to end—17 (18, 20, 21, 23, 24) sts each Front. Work even for 1 row.

NEXT ROW (RS): CO 20 (21, 22, 23, 23, 23) sts at each neck edge—37 (39, 42, 44, 46, 47) sts. Work even through Row 6 of pattern. Change to St st; work even until armhole measures same as for Back to beginning of armhole shaping. Shape armholes as for Back—38 (42, 46, 48, 51, 54) sts. Break yarn for Right Front.

BODY

Join Back and Fronts

NEXT ROW (RS): With RS facing, transfer Back sts, then Right Front sts to left-hand end of longer circ needle. Your sts should now be in the following order, from right to left, with RS facing: Left Front, Back, Right Front. Work across Left Front, CO 0 (0, 0, 4, 6, 8) sts for underarm, place marker for side at center of CO sts (between Front and Back for first 3 sizes), work 62 (70, 78, 82, 88, 94) sts for Back, pm, CO 0 (0, 0, 4, 6, 8) sts for underarm, place marker for side at center of CO sts, work to end—138 (154, 170, 186, 202, 218) sts. Work even until piece measures 12" from underarm, ending with a WS row.

Shape Hips

NEXT ROW (RS): Increase 4 sts this row, then every 12 rows twice, as follows: [Knit to 3 sts before marker, k2tog, k1, sm, k1, ssk] twice, knit to end—150 (166, 182, 198, 214, 230) sts. Work even, removing markers on first row, until piece measures 23" from underarm, ending with a WS row, decreasing 2 sts evenly on last row—148 (164, 180, 196, 212, 228) sts. Change to 2x2 Rib for Body; work even for 2". BO all sts in pattern.

SLEEVES

With RS facing, using shorter circ needle and beginning at center of underarm, pick up and knit 58 (62, 66, 70, 76, 82) sts evenly around armhole. Join for working in the rnd; pm for beginning of rnd.

Shape Cap

Note: Cap will be shaped using short rows (see Special Techniques, page 153); hide wraps as you come to them.

SHORT ROW 1 (RS): Work 40 (42, 44, 48, 51, 54) sts, wrp-t.

SHORT ROW 2 (WS): Work 22 (22, 22, 26, 26, 26) sts, wrp-t.

SHORT ROWS 3–30 (34, 38, 38, 42, 46): Work to wrapped st of row before previous row, wrp-t—4 (4, 4, 5, 6) sts remain unworked on either side of underarm marker. Change to working in the rnd; work even for 1 rnd, ending final rnd 2 sts before beginning of next rnd.

Shape Sleeve

Note: Change to dpns if necessary for number of sts on needle. Each Sleeve shaping rnd begins 2 sts before beginning-of-rnd marker.

WOODGRAIN II

RIGHT WOODGRAIN II

LEFT WOODGRAIN II

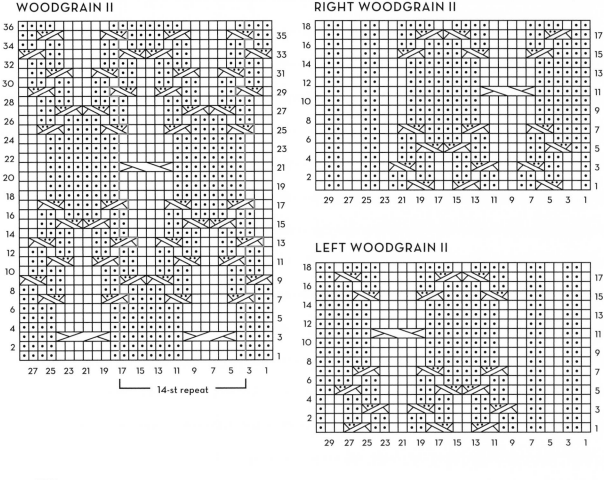

14-st repeat

KEY

☐ Knit on RS, purl on WS

⊡ Purl on RS, knit on WS

▨ 1/2 LC

▨ 1/2 RC

▨ 3/3 LC

▨ 3/3 RC

| Pattern repeat

NEXT RND: Decrease 2 sts this rnd, then every 2 (2, 2, 4 , 4, 4) rnds 8 (8, 8, 10, 11, 14) times, working decreases on last 2 sts of rnd and first 2 sts of next rnd, as follows: K2tog, sm, ssk, knit to end—40 (44, 48, 48, 52, 52) sts remain. Work even until piece measures 13¼ (13¾, 14¼, 14½, 14¾, 14¾)" from underarm, ending final rnd 2 sts before beginning of next rnd.

Shape Bottom of Sleeve

NEXT RND: Decrease 2 sts this rnd, then every other rnd 3 times, as follows: K2tog, sm, ssk, knit to end—32 (36, 40, 40, 44, 44) sts remain. Change to 2x2 Rib for Sleeve; work even for 4½". BO all sts in pattern.

FINISHING

Collar

With RS facing, using longer circ needle, pick up and knit 20 (21, 22, 23, 23, 23) sts from CO sts for Right Front neck, 8 (9, 11, 9, 10, 10) sts to shoulder, 32 (34, 36, 38, 40, 40) sts from Back sts, 8 (9, 11, 9, 10, 10) sts to Left Front CO sts, 20 (21, 22, 23, 23, 23) sts from Left Front CO sts—88 (94, 102, 102, 106, 106) sts. Break yarn and slide sts back to right-hand end of needle. With RS still facing, rejoin yarn; k0 (3, 0, 0, 2, 2), work 30 sts of Right Woodgrain II (from text or Chart), 28 (28, 42, 42, 42, 42) sts of Woodgrain II (from text or Chart), beginning with Row 5, then 30 sts of Left Woodgrain II (from text or Chart), k0 (3, 0, 0, 2, 2). Work even until Right and Left Woodgrain II patterns are complete, keeping sts at beginning and end of row (if applicable) in St st. BO all sts in pattern.

With RS facing, using crochet hook, work single crochet (sc) (see Special Techniques, page 156) along Left Front and Right Front edges, working 2 sts in every 3 rows.

Weave in ends. Block as desired.

Cut 2 pieces of twill tape 1" longer than Front edges. Fold under ½" at either end to WS, then sew one tape to RS of Left Front edge, and one to WS of Right Front edge. Sew one half of 9 snaps to twill tape on WS of Right Front, the first ¾" from top edge, the last 5" from bottom edge, and the remaining 7 evenly spaced between. Sew remaining half to RS of Left Front, opposite first half, approximately 1¼" in from edge.

suede-shoulder jacket

Wool pairs beautifully with suede, and I was pleased by the results I achieved when I used a piece of suede for the saddle portion of this jacket. I punched small holes into the edges of the suede and simply knitted into the holes. The double zipper adds styling options (sometimes it's just nice when sitting to be able to open your jacket from the bottom up) and the cotton twill tape lining the inside collar provides extra polish.

STITCH PATTERN

Rosette Stitch
(even number of sts; 4-row repeat)

ROWS 1 AND 3 (RS): Knit.

ROW 2: *P2tog, leaving sts on needle, k2tog into same 2 sts, slipping sts from needle together; repeat from * to end.

ROW 4: P1, *p2tog, leaving sts on needle, k2tog into same 2 sts, slipping sts from needle together; repeat from * to last st, p1.

Repeat Rows 1-4 for Rosette Stitch.

2x2 Rib for Sleeves
(multiple of 4 sts; 1-rnd repeat)

ALL RNDS: P1, *k2, p2; repeat from * to last 3 sts, k2, p1.

2x2 Rib for Body
(multiple of 4 sts; 1-row repeat)

ROW 1 (WS): P3, *k2, p2; repeat from * to last st, p1.

ROW 2: Knit the knit sts and purl the purl sts as they face you.

Repeat Row 2 for 2x2 Rib for Body.

sizes
Small (Medium, Large, X-Large, 2X-Large, 3X-Large)

finished measurements
35 1/2 (39 3/4, 44 1/4, 48 3/4, 52 1/2, 56 3/4)" bust, including zipper

yarn
Brooklyn Tweed Shelter (100% wool; 140 yards / 50 grams): 8 (9, 10, 11, 11, 12) hanks Sweatshirt

needles
One 24" (60 cm) long or longer circular (circ) needle size US 8 (5 mm)

One 16" (40 cm) long circular needle size US 6 (4 mm)

One set of five double-pointed needles (dpn) size US 6 (4 mm)

Change needle size if necessary to obtain correct gauge.

notions
Crochet hook size US E/4 (3.5 mm); one 23" x 16" piece of suede or leather; leather hole punch; waste yarn; stitch marker; 24" long 1/2" wide coordinating cotton twill tape; 20 (20, 20, 22, 22, 22)" two-way separating zipper; sewing needle and matching thread

gauge
21 sts and 24 rows = 4" (10 cm) in Rosette Stitch, using larger needle

20 sts and 28 rows = 4" (10 cm) in 2x2 Rib for Sleeves, using smaller needle, slightly stretched

A piece of suede adds a bit of structure to the shoulders of this jacket.

NOTES

※ When picking up stitches, consider using a crochet hook to pick up the stitches, then place them on the needle. The crochet hook will go through the hole more easily than the needle will. When placing the stitches on the needle, make sure that they are not twisted.

※ When picking up stitches for the Sleeves, you will pick up in the corner holes of the Suede Shoulder Panel where stitches have already been picked up for the Front and Back. When picking up stitches for the Front Bands and Collar, you will pick up in the corner holes where stitches have already been picked up for the Fronts and Front Bands, respectively.

SUEDE SHOULDER PANEL

Make 2 photocopies or scans of the Shoulder template, enlarging them 400% so that bottom of template (half Back width) measures 7 ½ (7 ¾, 8 ¼, 8 ½, 9, 9 ½)" wide. Cut out template along lines for your size, then flip one template over and tape them together along the dotted line, to form the full Shoulder template [full Back width measures 15 (15 ½, 16 ½, 17, 18, 19)"]. Using template, cut out suede for your size. Mark ¼" spaces evenly around outside edge of entire piece, including neck opening, approximately ¼" in from all edges, referring to template for specific hole counts. Punch a hole in each space using the smallest hole setting.

BACK

With RS of Suede Shoulder Panel facing, using crochet hook, beginning at left-hand edge of Shoulder Panel, and working from left to right, pick up and knit 59 (61, 65, 67, 71, 75) sts in holes along Back edge of Shoulder, as indicated in Shoulder template, placing each st on larger circ needle as it is picked up. *Note: This will enable you to begin the st pattern with a RS row.*

INCREASE ROW (RS): K1 (2, 2, 3, 2, 2), *k1 (1, 2, 1, 2, 1), k1-f/b, [k2, k1-f/b] 2 (4, 9, 6, 10, 11) times; repeat from * 6 (3, 1, 2, 1, 1) time(s), [k1-f/b] 0 (1, 1, 2, 1, 1) time(s), k2—80 (82, 86, 90, 94, 100) sts. Change to Rosette Stitch, beginning with Row 2; work even for 7 (5, 5, 3, 3, 7) rows.

Shape Armholes

NEXT ROW (RS): Increase 2 sts each side this row, every 8 (6, 4, 4, 4, 2) rows 1 (1, 3, 3, 3, 6) time(s), then every 0 (4, 0, 2, 2, 0) rows 0 (1, 0, 1, 2, 0) time(s), as follows: When working Row 1 of Rosette Stitch, k1, M1-b/f, knit to last st, M1-b/f, k1; when working Row 3 of Rosette Stitch, k2, M1-b/f, knit to last 2 sts, M1-b/f, k2—88 (94, 102, 110, 118, 128) sts.

Work even for 1 row. Make note of row of Rosette Stitch on which you ended. Break yarn and transfer sts to waste yarn for Body.

RIGHT FRONT

With RS of Suede Shoulder Panel facing, using crochet hook and larger circ needle, beginning at left-hand corner of Right Front edge of Shoulder Panel, and working as for Back, pick up and knit 19 (20, 22, 23, 25, 27) sts in holes along Right Front edge of Shoulder Panel.

INCREASE ROW (RS): K1-f/b, k1 (1, 2, 0, 1, 1), *k1, k1-f/b, [k2, k1-f/b] 1 (1, 1, 1, 1, 3) time(s); repeat from * 2 (2, 2, 3, 3, 1) time(s), [k1-f/b] 0 (1, 1, 0, 0, 0) time(s), k2 (2, 3, 2, 3, 3)—26 (28, 30, 32, 34, 36). Change to Rosette Stitch, beginning with Row 2; work even for 7 (5, 5, 3, 3, 7) rows. Shape armhole as for Back, ending with same row of Rosette Stitch as for Back—30 (34, 38, 42, 46, 50) sts. Break yarn and transfer sts to waste yarn for Body.

LEFT FRONT

Work as for Right Front, reversing all shaping. Leave sts on needle.

BODY

JOIN BACK TO FRONTS (RS): With RS facing, transfer Back sts, then Right Front sts to left-hand end of larger circ needle. Your sts should now be in the following order, from right to left, with RS facing: Left Front, Back, Right Front. Using yarn attached to Left Front, work across Left Front sts, CO 6 (10, 14, 18, 20, 22) sts for underarm, work to end of Back, CO 6 (10, 14, 18, 20, 22) sts for underarm, work to end—160 (182, 206, 230, 250, 272) sts. Work even until piece measures 11 (11, 11, 11½, 11½, 11½)" from underarm, ending with a WS row. Break yarn and transfer sts to waste yarn for Bottom Band.

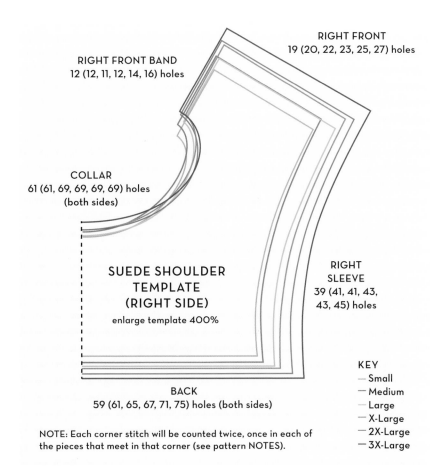

RIGHT FRONT
19 (20, 22, 23, 25, 27) holes

RIGHT FRONT BAND
12 (12, 11, 12, 14, 16) holes

COLLAR
61 (61, 69, 69, 69, 69) holes
(both sides)

SUEDE SHOULDER
TEMPLATE
(RIGHT SIDE)
enlarge template 400%

RIGHT
SLEEVE
39 (41, 41, 43, 43, 45) holes

KEY
— Small
— Medium
— Large
— X-Large
— 2X-Large
— 3X-Large

BACK
59 (61, 65, 67, 71, 75) holes (both sides)

NOTE: Each corner stitch will be counted twice, once in each of the pieces that meet in that corner (see pattern NOTES).

SLEEVES

With RS facing, using smaller circ needle and beginning at center of underarm, pick up and knit 17 (18, 20, 21, 23, 22) sts to Suede Shoulder Panel, 39 (41, 41, 43, 43, 45) sts along Suede Shoulder Panel, then 16 (17, 19, 20, 22, 21) sts to center of underarm—72 (76, 80, 84, 88, 88) sts. Join for working in the rnd; pm for beginning of rnd, and place 1 cap-shaping marker on either side of sts picked up from sts CO for underarm.

Shape Cap

Note: Sleeve Cap will be shaped using short rows (see Special Techniques, page 153); hide wraps as you come to them.

SHORT ROW 1 (RS): Begin 2x2 Rib for Sleeves; work 48 (50, 52, 54, 56, 56) sts, wrp-t.

SHORT ROW 2 (WS): Work 24 sts, wrp-t.

SHORT ROWS 3–22 (26, 30, 30, 34, 34): Work to 1 st past wrapped st of row before previous row, wrp-t. *Note: You may go 1 st past cap-shaping marker if necessary to complete a repeat.*

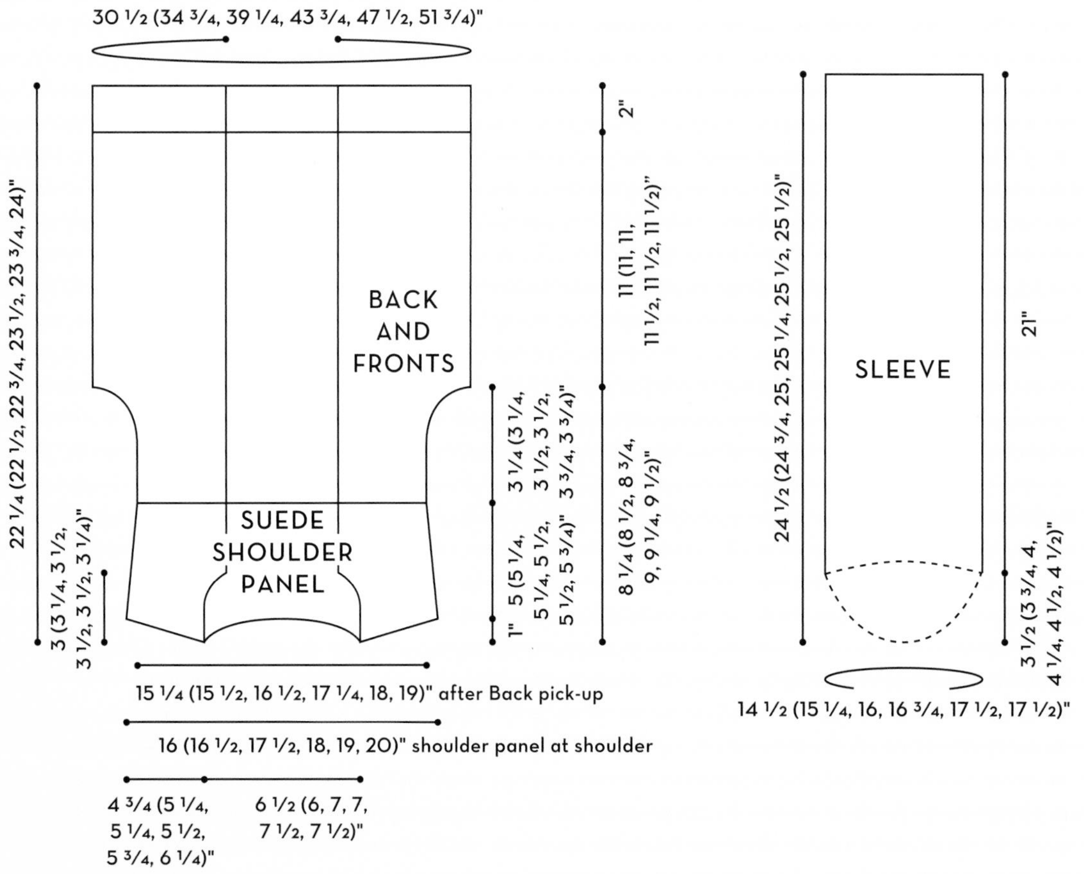

30 1/2 (34 3/4, 39 1/4, 43 3/4, 47 1/2, 51 3/4)"
2"
11 (11, 11, 11 1/2, 11 1/2, 11 1/2)"
BACK AND FRONTS
22 1/4 (22 1/2, 22 3/4, 23 1/2, 23 3/4, 24)"
3 (3 1/4, 3 1/2, 3 1/2, 3 1/2, 3 1/4)"
1"
5 (5 1/4, 5 1/4, 5 1/2, 5 1/2, 5 3/4)"
3 1/4 (3 1/4, 3 1/2, 3 1/2, 3 3/4, 3 3/4)"
8 1/4 (8 1/2, 8 3/4, 9, 9 1/4, 9 1/2)"
SUEDE SHOULDER PANEL
15 1/4 (15 1/2, 16 1/2, 17 1/4, 18, 19)" after Back pick-up
16 (16 1/2, 17 1/2, 18, 19, 20)" shoulder panel at shoulder
4 3/4 (5 1/4, 5 1/4, 5 1/2, 5 3/4, 6 1/4)"
6 1/2 (6, 7, 7, 7 1/2, 7 1/2)"
24 1/2 (24 3/4, 25, 25 1/4, 25 1/2, 25 1/2)"
SLEEVE
21"
3 1/2 (3 3/4, 4, 4 1/4, 4 1/2, 4 1/2)"
14 1/2 (15 1/4, 16, 16 3/4, 17 1/2, 17 1/2)"

NEXT RND (RS): Change to working in the rnd; work even until piece measures 21" from underarm. BO all sts in pattern.

FINISHING

Front Bands

With RS facing, using larger circ needle, pick up and knit 88 (88, 90, 92, 96, 100) sts along Right Front edge, including 12 (12, 11, 12, 14, 16) sts from holes in Suede Shoulder Panel. Break yarn; do not turn. Slide sts back to right-hand end of needle. Begin Rosette Stitch; work even for 2", ending with a WS row. BO all sts knitwise.

Bottom Ribbing

Transfer Body sts to larger circ needle. With RS facing, beginning at lower edge of Left Front Band, pick up and knit 9 sts across Band, work across Body sts, pick up and knit 9 sts across Right Front Band—178 (200, 224, 248, 268, 290) sts Begin 2x2 Rib for Body; work even for 2", ending with a WS row. BO all sts in pattern.

Collar

With RS facing, using larger circ needle, pick up and knit 10 sts from Right Front Band, 61 (61, 69, 69, 69, 69) sts around neck opening from holes in Suede Shoulder Panel, then 9 sts from Left Front Band—80 (80, 88, 88, 88, 88) sts.

INCREASE ROW (RS): K4 (4, 0, 0, 0, 0), [k3, k1-f/b] 18 (18, 22, 22, 22, 22) times, k4 (4, 0, 0, 0, 0)—98 (98, 110, 110, 110, 110) sts. Begin 2x2 Rib for Body; work even for 1 row, placing marker at center Back neck.

Shape Collar

Note: Collar will be shaped using short rows (see Special Techniques, page 153). Work wraps together with wrapped sts as you come to them.

SHORT ROW 1 (RS): Continuing in 2x2 Rib, work to 8 sts past center Back neck marker, wrp-t.

SHORT ROW 2 (WS): Work 16 sts, wrp-t.

SHORT ROWS 3-4: Work to 7 sts past wrapped st of row before previous row, wrp-t.

Repeat Short Rows 3 and 4 until you have 7 (7, 11, 11, 11, 11) sts between final wrapped st and end of row on each side.

NEXT ROW (RS): Work across all sts for 2 rows. BO all sts in pattern.

Using crochet hook, beginning at Left Front Bottom Band, work single crochet (sc) (see Special Techniques, page 156) around Left Front Band, Collar, and Right Front Band.

Using sewing needle and matching thread, sew in zipper. Cut twill tape long enough to fit top edge of collar, plus 1". Fold under ½" at either end and sew to WS of top edge of Collar.

Weave in all ends. Block as desired. *Note: To block the knitted portions while keeping the leather dry, turn Jacket inside out and, using a layer of cotton cloth between Jacket and iron, press lightly on steam setting.*

homage cable sweater

The cable combination I used for the front and back (body portions) of this piece came from a sweater my grandpa used to wear when I was a child. In a favorite photo of him, he is wearing it and I am three years old, sitting on his lap. In graduate school, I spent months working to re-create the sweater and still frequently wear the replica I finished (although now all I notice are the unnecessary seams that came from working it in pieces from the bottom up). For this new top-down version, I chose Walker's Wave of Honey Cable stitch pattern (from *A Treasury of Knitting Patterns*), which matches the body perfectly, is deceptively easy to knit, and helps echo the heirloom feeling of the original.

ABBREVIATIONS

3/3 LC: Slip 3 sts to cn, hold to front, k3, k3 from cn.

3/3 RC: Slip 3 sts to cn, hold to back, k3, k3 from cn.

LT: Knit into back of second st, then knit first and second sts together through back loop; slip both sts from left-hand needle together.

LT-tbl: Slip 1 st to cn, hold to front, p1, k1-tbl from cn.

RT: K2tog, but do not drop sts from left-hand needle; insert right-hand needle between 2 sts just worked and knit first st again, then slip both sts from left-hand needle together.

RT-tbl: Slip 1 st to cn, hold to back, k1-tbl, p1 from cn.

sizes
Small (Medium, Large, 1X-Large, 2X-Large)

finished measurements
34 ¾ (39 ¼, 42 ¼, 47, 50 ¾)" bust

yarn
Jill Draper Makes Stuff Hudson (100% superwash merino; 245 yards / 100 grams): 8 (8, 9, 10, 11) hanks Sterling

needles
One 29" (70 cm) long or longer circular (circ) needle size US 7 (4.5 mm)

One 16" (40 cm) long circular needle size US 7 (4.5 mm)

One set of five double-pointed needles (dpn) size US 7 (4.5 mm)

Change needle size if necessary to obtain correct gauge.

notions
Crochet hook size US F/5 (3.75 mm); stitch markers; waste yarn

gauge
20 sts and 28 rows = 4" (10 cm) in Stockinette stitch (St st)

34 sts and 26 rows = 4" (10 cm) in Wave of Honey Cable Flat

27 sts and 29 rows = 4" (10 cm) in Center Cable Panel Flat

STITCH PATTERNS

Wave of Honey Cable Flat

(multiple of 6 sts + 2; 4-row repeat)

ROW 1 (RS): P2, *LT, RT, p2; repeat from * to end.

ROW 2: K2, *p4, k2; repeat from * to end.

ROW 3: P2, *RT, LT, p2; repeat from * to end.

ROW 4: Repeat Row 2.

Repeat Rows 1-4 for Wave of Honey Cable Flat.

Wave of Honey Cable in the Rnd

(multiple of 6 sts + 2; 4-rnd repeat)

RND 1: P2, *LT, RT, p2; repeat from * to end.

RND 2: P2, *k4, p2; repeat from * to end.

RND 3: P2, *RT, LT, p2; repeat from * to end.

RND 4: Repeat Rnd 2.

Repeat Rnds 1-4 for Wave of Honey Cable in the Rnd.

Wavy Rib Flat

(panel of 2 sts; 4-row repeat)

ROWS 1 AND 3 (WS): P2.

ROW 2: RT.

ROW 4: LT.

Repeat Rows 1-4 for Wavy Rib Flat.

Twist and Moss Cable Flat (see Chart)

(panel of 21 sts; 16-row repeat)

ROW 1 (WS): K6, [p1-tbl, k1] twice, p1, [k1, p1-tbl] twice, k6.

ROW 2: P5, [RT-tbl] twice, k1, p1, k1, [LT-tbl] twice, p5.

ROWS 3 AND 15: K5, p1-tbl, k1, p1-tbl, [k1, p1] twice, [k1, p1-tbl] twice, k5.

ROW 4: P4, [RT-tbl] twice, [k1, p1] twice, k1, [LT-tbl] twice, p4.

ROWS 5 AND 13: K4, p1-tbl, k1, p1-tbl, [k1, p1] 3 times, [k1, p1-tbl] twice, k4.

ROW 6: P3, [RT-tbl] twice, [k1, p1] 3 times, k1, [LT-tbl] twice, p3.

ROWS 7 AND 11: K3, p1-tbl, k1, p1-tbl, [k1, p1] 4 times, [k1, p1-tbl] twice, k3.

ROW 8: P2, [RT-tbl] twice, [k1, p1] 4 times, k1, [LT-tbl] twice, p2.

ROW 9: K2, p1-tbl, k1, p1-tbl, [k1, p1] 5 times, [k1, p1-tbl] twice, k2.

ROW 10: P2, [LT-tbl] twice, [p1, k1] 4 times, p1, [RT-tbl] twice, p2.

ROW 12: P3, [LT-tbl] twice, [p1, k1] 3 times, p1, [RT-tbl] twice, p3.

ROW 14: P4, [LT-tbl] twice, [p1, k1] twice, p1, [RT-tbl] twice, p4.

ROW 16: P5, [LT-tbl] twice, p1, k1, p1, [RT-tbl] twice, p5.

Repeat Rows 1-16 for Twist and Moss Cable Flat.

Twist and Moss Cable in the Rnd (see Chart)
(panel of 21 sts; 16-rnd repeat)

RND 1: P6, [k1-tbl, p1] twice, k1, [p1, k1-tbl] twice, p6.

RND 2: P5, [RT-tbl] twice, k1, p1, k1, [LT-tbl] twice, p5.

RNDS 3 AND 15: P5, [k1-tbl, p1] twice, [k1, p1] twice, [k1-tbl, p1] twice, p4.

RND 4: P4, [RT-tbl] twice, [k1, p1] twice, k1, [LT-tbl] twice, p4.

RNDS 5 AND 13: P4, [k1-tbl, p1] twice, [k1, p1] 3 times, [k1-tbl, p1] twice, p3.

RND 6: P3, [RT-tbl] twice, [k1, p1] 3 times, k1, [LT-tbl] twice, p3.

RND 7 AND 11: P3, [k1-tbl, p1] twice, [k1, p1] 4 times, [k1-tbl, p1] twice, p2.

RND 8: P2, [RT-tbl] twice, [k1, p1] 4 times, k1, [LT-tbl] twice, p2.

RND 9: P2, [k1-tbl, p1] twice, [k1, p1] 5 times, [k1-tbl, p1] twice, p1.

RND 10: P2, [LT-tbl] twice, [p1, k1] 4 times, p1, [RT-tbl] twice, p2.

RND 12: P3, [LT-tbl] twice, [p1, k1] 3 times, p1, [RT-tbl] twice, p3.

RND 14: P4, [LT-tbl] twice, [p1, k1] twice, p1, [RT-tbl] twice, p4.

RND 16: P5, [LT-tbl] twice, p1, k1, p1, [RT-tbl] twice, p5.

Repeat Rnds 1–16 for Twist and Moss Cable in the Rnd.

Center Cable Panel Flat (see Chart)
[panel of 44 (50, 50, 56, 56) sts; 8-row repeat]

ROW 1 AND ALL WS ROWS (WS): P4, k2, p6, k2, [p1, k2] 6 (8, 8, 10, 10) times, p6, k2, p4.

TWIST AND MOSS CABLE

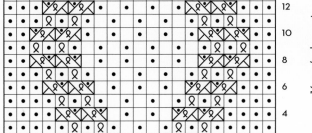

21 19 17 15 13 11 9 7 5 3 1

16-row/rnd repeat

16 14 12 10 8 6 4 2

KEY

☐ Knit on RS, purl on WS

• Purl on RS, knit on WS

Ⴍ K1-tbl on RS, p1-tbl on WS

⧅ RT

⧄ LT

⧅ RT-tbl

⧄ LT-tbl

⬡ 3/3 LC

⬡ 3/3 RC

ROWS 2 AND 6: RT, LT, p2, k6, [p2, k1-tbl] 6 (8, 8, 10, 10) times, p2, k6, p2, RT, LT.

ROW 4: LT, RT, p2, 3/3 LC, [p2, k1-tbl] 6 (8, 8, 10, 10) times, p2, 3/3 RC, p2, LT, RT.

ROW 8: LT, RT, p2, k6, [p2, k1-tbl] 6 (8, 8, 10, 10) times, p2, k6, p2, LT, RT.
Repeat Rows 1-8 for Center Cable Panel Flat.

Center Cable Panel in the Rnd (see Chart)
[panel of 44 (50, 50, 56, 56) sts; 8-rnd repeat]

RND 1 AND ALL ODD-NUMBERED RNDS: K4, p2, k6, [p2, k1] 6 (8, 8, 10, 10) times, p2, k6, p2, k4.

RNDS 2 AND 6: RT, LT, p2, k6, [p2, k1-tbl] 6 (8, 8, 10, 10) times, p2, k6, p2, RT, LT.

RND 4: LT, RT, p2, 3/3 LC, [p2, k1-tbl] 6 (8, 8, 10, 10) times, p2, 3/3 RC, p2, LT, RT.

RND 8: LT, RT, p2, k6, [p2, k1-tbl] 6 (8, 8, 10, 10) times, p2, k6, p2, LT, RT.
Repeat Rnds 1-8 for Center Cable Panel in the Rnd.

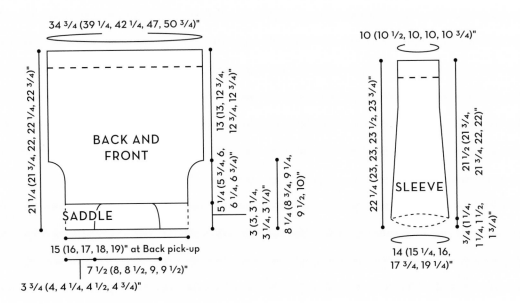

CENTER CABLE PANEL

8-row/rnd repeat

29 27 25 23 21 19 17 15 13 11 9 7 5 3 1

work these 3 sts 6 (8, 8, 10, 10) times

34 3/4 (39 1/4, 42 1/4, 47, 50 3/4)"

BACK AND FRONT

SADDLE

21 1/4 (21 3/4, 22, 22 1/4, 22 3/4)"

13 (13, 12 3/4, 12 3/4, 12 3/4)"

5 1/4 (5 3/4, 6, 6 1/4, 6 3/4)"

3 (3, 3 1/4, 3 1/4, 3 1/4)"

8 1/4 (8 3/4, 9 1/4, 9 1/2, 10)"

15 (16, 17, 18, 19)" at Back pick-up

7 1/2 (8, 8 1/2, 9, 9 1/2)"

3 3/4 (4, 4 1/4, 4 1/2, 4 3/4)"

10 (10 1/2, 10, 10, 10 3/4)"

SLEEVE

22 1/4 (23, 23, 23 1/2, 23 3/4)"

21 1/2 (21 3/4, 21 3/4, 22, 22)"

3/4 (1 1/4, 1 1/2, 1 3/4)"

14 (15 1/4, 16, 17 3/4, 19 1/4)"

Twisted Rib

(even number of sts; 2-rnd repeat)

RND 1: *K1, p1; repeat from * to end.

RND 2: *K1-tbl, p1; repeat from * to end.

Repeat Rnds 1 and 2 for Twisted Rib.

LEFT SADDLE

Using crochet hook, waste yarn, and Provisional CO (see Special Techniques, page 155), CO 26 (26, 32, 32, 32) sts. Change to working yarn and longer circ needle. Begin Wave of Honey Cable Flat; work even until piece measures 3¾ (4, 4¼, 4½, 4¾)" from the beginning, ending with a WS row.

Shape Front Neck

NEXT ROW (RS): CO 2 sts at beginning of this and next RS row once, then CO 20 sts at beginning of following RS row, working CO sts in St st until you have enough sts to work in Wave of Honey Cable—50 (50, 56, 56, 56) sts. Work even until piece measures 7½ (8, 8½, 9, 9½)" from the beginning, ending with a WS row; make note of last row worked. Break yarn, transfer sts to waste yarn, and set aside.

RIGHT SADDLE

With WS facing, carefully unravel Provisional CO and place sts on shorter circ needle for Right Saddle. Mark edge for center Back neck. Begin Wave of Honey Cable Flat, beginning with Row 4; work even until piece measures 3¾ (4, 4¼, 4½, 4¾)" from marker, ending with a WS row.

Shape Front Neck

NEXT ROW (RS): CO 2 sts at end of this and next RS row once, then CO 20 sts at end of following RS row, working CO sts in St st until you have enough to work in Wave of Honey Cable—50 (50, 56, 56, 56) sts. Work even until piece measures 7½ (8, 8½, 9, 9½)" from marker, ending with a WS row; make note of last row worked. Break yarn, transfer sts to waste yarn, and set aside.

FRONT

With RS of Saddle facing, using longer circ needle and beginning at live Right Saddle sts, pick up and knit 24 (26, 28, 30, 32) sts along side edge to CO edge; join a second ball of yarn, beginning at CO sts for Left Neck, pick up and knit 24 (26, 28, 30, 32) sts along side edge to live Left Saddle sts.

SET-UP ROW (WS): Working BOTH SIDES AT THE SAME TIME using separate balls of yarn, for left neck edge, p1 (edge st, keep in St st), work 0 (1, 3, 4, 6) sts in St st, work 2 sts of Wavy Rib Flat, beginning with Row 3, then work 21 sts of Twist and Moss Cable Flat, work 0 (1, 1, 2, 2) sts in St st; for right neck edge, work 0 (1, 1, 2, 2) sts in St st, work 21 sts of Twist and Moss Cable Flat, work 2 sts of Wavy Rib Flat, beginning with Row 1, work 0 (1, 3, 4, 6) sts in St st, p1 (edge st, keep in St st).

Shape Neck

NEXT ROW (RS): Continuing in patterns as established, CO 1 st at each neck edge this row, then every other row 1 (1, 1, 2, 2) time(s), working CO sts in St st as they become available—26 (28, 30, 33, 35) sts each side. Work even for 1 row. Break yarn for left side.

NEXT ROW (RS): Work across right Front sts, CO 40 (44, 44, 46, 46) sts for Front neck, work across left side—92 (100, 104, 112, 116) sts.

NEXT ROW: Work 24 (25, 27, 28, 30) sts as established, work 44 (50, 50, 56, 56) sts from Center Cable Panel Flat, work to end as established. Work even until piece measures 3 (3¼, 3¼, 3¼, 3½)" from pick-up row, ending with a WS row; make note of last row worked.

Shape Armholes

INCREASE ROW (RS): Continuing in patterns as established, increase 1 st each side this row, then every other row 7 (8, 9, 10, 11) times, as follows, working increased sts in St st as they become available: K1, M1-R, work to last st, M1-L, k1—108 (118, 124, 134, 140) sts. Work even for 1 row. Break yarn, transfer sts to waste yarn, and set aside.

BACK

With RS of Saddle facing, using longer circ needle and beginning at Left Saddle live sts, pick up and knit 92 (100, 104, 112, 116) sts along side edge of Saddle to Right Saddle live sts. Break yarn. Slide sts back to right-hand end of needle.

SET-UP ROW (WS): P1 (edge st, keep in St st), work 0 (1, 3, 4, 6) sts in St st, work 2 sts of Wavy Rib Flat, beginning with Row 3, 21 sts of Twist and Moss Cable Flat, 44 (50, 50, 56, 56) sts of Center Cable Panel Flat, 21 sts of Twist and Moss Cable Flat, 2 sts of Wavy Rib Flat, beginning with Row 1, work 0 (1, 3, 4, 6) sts in St st, p1 (edge st, keep in St st). Work even until piece measures 3 (3¼, 3¼, 3¼, 3½)" from pick-up row, ending with same row as for Front. Shape armholes as for Front—108 (118, 124, 134, 140) sts.

BODY

Join Back and Front

With RS facing, transfer Front sts to left-hand end of circ needle. Work across Back, CO 0 (2, 6, 8, 12) sts for underarm, pm for side at center of CO sts (between Front and Back for size S) then across Front, CO 0 (2, 6, 8, 12) sts for underarm, pm for side and beginning of rnd at center of CO sts—216 (240, 260, 284, 304) sts. Join for working in the rnd. Continuing to work all patterns as established, change to working in the rnd; work even until piece measures 11 (11, 10¾, 10¾, 10¼)" from underarm. Purl 1 rnd.

RIBBING SET-UP RND: *[K1-tbl, p1] 15 (17, 19, 22, 24) times, k1-tbl, p2tog, [k1-tbl, p1] 2 (2, 3, 3, 4) times, k1-tbl, p2tog, [k1-tbl, p1] 1 (3, 2, 2, 1) time(s), [k1-tbl, p2tog] 5 times, [k1-tbl, p1] 2 (2, 3, 3, 4) times, [(k1-tbl, p1) twice, k1-tbl, p2tog] twice, [k1-tbl, p1] 15 (17, 19, 22, 24) times, k1-tbl, p2tog; repeat from * once—196 (220, 240, 264, 284) sts remain. Change to Twisted Rib; work even for 2". BO all sts in pattern.

SLEEVES

Transfer sts for Left Saddle to shorter circ needle. With RS facing, using shorter circ needle and beginning at center of underarm, pick up and knit 20 (23, 24, 28, 32) sts to Left Saddle, pm, work across 50 (50, 56, 56, 56) Saddle sts in Wave of Honey Cable Flat, beginning with row after last row worked, pm, pick up and knit 20 (23, 24, 28, 32) sts to center underarm—90 (96, 104, 112, 120) sts. Join for working in the rnd; pm for beginning of rnd.

Shape Cap

Note: Cap is shaped using short rows (see Special Techniques, page 153).

SHORT ROW 1 (RS): Continuing to work Wave of Honey Cable Flat between markers, and working remaining sts in St st, work to 5 (4, 4, 3, 3) sts after second marker, wrp-t.

SHORT ROW 2 (WS): Work to 5 sts after first marker, wrp-t.

SHORT ROWS 3–6 (8, 8, 10, 12): Work to 4 sts past wrapped st of row before previous row, hiding wrap as you come to it, wrp-t. Work to end, hiding wrap as you come to it.

NEXT RND: Change to working in the rnd, working Wave of Honey Cable in the Rnd between markers, beginning with rnd after last row worked, and St st on remaining sts. Work even for 1", ending final rnd 2 sts before beginning of next rnd.

Shape Sleeve

Note: Each Sleeve shaping rnd begins 2 sts before beginning-of-rnd marker. Change to dpns when necessary for number of sts on needle.

DECREASE RND: Decrease 2 sts this rnd, every other rnd 1 (1, 2, 4, 6) time(s), every 6 rnds 3 (7, 7, 5, 8) times, then every 12 (12, 12, 8, 8) rnds 5 (3, 4, 7, 5) times, working decreases on last 2 sts of rnd and first 2 sts of next rnd, as follows: K2tog, sm, ssk, work to end—70 (72, 76, 78, 80) sts remain. Work even until piece measures 19 ½ (19 ¾, 19 ¾, 20, 20)" from underarm. Purl 1 rnd, ending 1 st before beginning of next rnd.

RIBBING SET-UP RND: P2tog, repositioning marker to after decreased st, [k1-tbl, p1] 4 (5, 6, 7, 7) times, k1-tbl, [p2tog, k1-tbl] 17 times, [k1-tbl, p1] 4 (4, 5, 5, 6) times—52 (54, 58, 60, 62) sts remain. Change to Twisted Rib; work even for 2".

FINISHING

Collar

With RS facing, using shorter circ needle and beginning at center Back neck, pick up and knit 1 st in each CO st and 2 sts for every 3 rows around neck opening. Join for working in the rnd; pm for beginning of rnd. Purl 1 rnd. Begin Twisted Rib; work even for 1". BO all sts in pattern.

Weave in ends. Block as desired.

The top-down saddle shoulder template presents infinite design possibilities. For this sweater, I liked being able to run horizontal lines of the Waves of Honey Cable across the back.

spring tree sweater

This colorway of Malabrigo's Arroyo reminds me of a walk in the woods after it's rained. Though I had never designed with (or even been drawn to) variegated yarn before, this soft, gorgeous wool changed my mind instantly. I also had my doubts about kimono sleeves, concerned that (whatever my design) too much material under the arms might create an unflattering "flying squirrel" effect. But the beautiful drape of the knitted Malabrigo quickly helped put my concerns to rest, and keeping the neckline low provided a flattering counterpoint to the fullness of the sleeves.

ABBREVIATION

MR (make ringlet): P2, slip these 2 sts back to left-hand needle wyif, bring yarn in front of the 2 sts and between needles to back, slip sts back to right-hand needle; bring yarn to front again if next st to be worked is a purl st; leave yarn in back if next st to be worked is a knit st.

STITCH PATTERNS

Ringlet Stitch
(even number of sts; 2-row repeat)
ROW 1 (RS): K1, *MR; repeat from * to last st, k1.
ROW 2: Purl.
Repeat Rows 1 and 2 for Ringlet Stitch.

1x1 Rib
(even number of sts; 1-rnd repeat)
ALL RNDS: *K1, p1; repeat from * to end.

sizes
X-Small (Small, Medium, Large, 1X-Large, 2X-Large)

To fit bust sizes 28–30 (32–34, 36–38, 40–42, 44–46, 48–50)"

finished measurements
32 (35 ¾, 39 ½, 43 ½, 47 ¼, 51)" waist

yarn
Malabrigo Yarn Arroyo (100% superwash merino wool; 335 yards / 100 grams): 4 (4, 4, 5, 5, 6) hanks Chircas

needles
One 29" (70 cm) long or longer circular (circ) needle size US 5 (3.75 mm)

Change needle size if necessary to obtain correct gauge.

notions
Crochet hook size US E/4 (3.5 mm); waste yarn; stitch markers

gauge
25 sts and 36 rows = 4" (10 cm) in Stockinette stitch (St st)

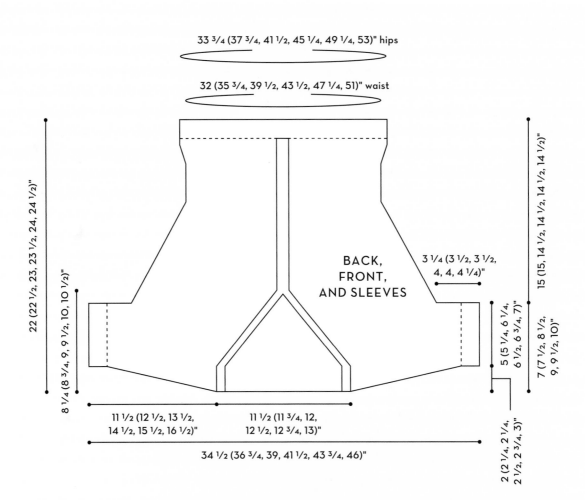

33 3/4 (37 3/4, 41 1/2, 45 1/4, 49 1/4, 53)" hips

32 (35 3/4, 39 1/2, 43 1/2, 47 1/4, 51)" waist

22 (22 1/2, 23, 23 1/2, 24, 24 1/2)"

8 1/4 (8 3/4, 9, 9 1/2, 10, 10 1/2)"

BACK,
FRONT,
AND SLEEVES

3 1/4 (3 1/2, 3 1/2, 4, 4, 4 1/4)"

15 (15, 14 1/2, 14 1/2, 14 1/2, 14 1/2)"

5 (5 1/4, 6 1/4, 6 1/2, 6 3/4, 7)"

7 (7 1/2, 8 1/2, 9, 9 1/2, 10)"

11 1/2 (12 1/2, 13 1/2, 14 1/2, 15 1/2, 16 1/2)"

11 1/2 (11 3/4, 12, 12 1/2, 12 3/4, 13)"

2 (2 1/4, 2 1/4, 2 1/2, 2 3/4, 3)"

34 1/2 (36 3/4, 39, 41 1/2, 43 3/4, 46)"

BACK/SLEEVES

Using crochet hook, waste yarn, and Provisional CO (see Special Techniques, page 155), CO 217 (231, 245, 261, 275, 289) sts. Change to circ needle and working yarn.

NEXT ROW (RS): Work 10 sts in Ringlet Stitch, work in St st to last 10 sts, work in Ringlet Stitch to end. Work even for 1 row.

NEXT ROW (RS): Work 10 sts in Ringlet Stitch, k63 (69, 75, 82, 88, 94), pm, k71 (73, 75, 77, 79, 81), pm, knit to last 10 sts, work in Ringlet Stitch to end.

Shape Shoulders
Note: Shoulders are shaped using short rows (see Special Techniques, page 153).

SHORT ROWS 1 (WS) AND 2: Work to second marker, sm, work 6 (4, 10, 9, 7, 5) sts, wrp-t.

SHORT ROWS 3–16 (18, 18, 20, 22, 24): Work to wrapped st from row before previous row, hide wrap, work 7 sts, wrp-t. Work even in patterns as established, hiding remaining wraps as you come to them, until armholes measure 5 (5¼, 6¼, 6½, 6¾, 7)" from the beginning, ending with a RS row. Break yarn and place sts on waste yarn.

RIGHT AND LEFT FRONT/SLEEVES

With RS facing, carefully unravel Provisional CO and place sts on circ needle for Front. Mark armhole edge for top of armhole.

NEXT ROW (RS): Rejoin yarn; pm to mark Sleeve edge, work 10 sts in Ringlet Stitch, work 63 (69, 75, 82, 88, 94) sts in St st, join a second ball of yarn, BO 71 (73, 75, 77, 79, 81), sts for Back neck, knit to last 10 sts, work in Ringlet Stitch to end—73 (79, 85, 92, 98, 104) sts remain each side. Working BOTH SIDES AT THE SAME TIME using separate balls of yarn, shape shoulders as for Back.

Shape Neck and Armholes
Note: Neck and armhole shaping will be worked at the same time; please read entire section through before beginning. Neck shaping will not be completed until after Front and Back are joined.

INCREASE ROWS (RS): Increase 1 st each neck edge this row, then every other row 28 (29, 30, 31, 32, 33) times, as follows: For Right Front, knit to last 2 sts, M1-L, k2; for Left Front, k2, M1-R, knit to end. *Note: When armhole shaping is complete, there are 96 (103, 113, 122, 129, 136) sts for each Front/Sleeve, if row gauge was matched exactly. You may have a few sts more or less at this point due to differences in row gauge and measuring.* AT THE SAME TIME, when piece measures 5 (5¼, 6¼, 6½, 6¾, 7)" from marker, ending with a RS row, join Fronts and Back as follows:

BODY

Join Fronts/Sleeves and Back/Sleeves
With RS facing, leave first 21 (22, 23, 25, 26, 27) sts of Right Front/Sleeve on needle; transfer remaining sts to waste yarn. Transfer corresponding 21 (22, 23, 25, 26, 27) sts of Back/Sleeves to opposite end of circ needle.

Using Kitchener Stitch (see Special Techniques, page 152), join Sleeves. Repeat for opposite Sleeve.

NEXT ROW (WS): With WS facing, transfer Right Front sts, pm, Back sts, pm, then Left Front sts to circ needle—325 (349, 379, 405, 429, 453) sts. *Note: You may have a few sts more or less at this point due to differences in row gauge and measuring.*

Shape Armholes

NEXT ROW (RS): Continuing to work neck shaping as established, decrease 4 sts this row, then every other row 35 times, as follows: [Knit to 2 sts before marker, k2tog, sm, ssk] twice—193 (217, 241, 265, 289, 313) sts remain after all shaping is complete. Work even until piece measures 11 ½ (11 ½, 11, 11, 10 ½, 10 ½)" from Sleeve join.

Shape Hips

NEXT ROW (RS): Increase 4 sts this row, then every 6 rows twice, as follows: [Knit to 10 sts before marker, M1-L, knit to 10 sts after marker, M1-R] twice, knit to end—205 (229, 253, 277, 301, 325) sts. Work even until piece measures 13 ½ (13 ½, 13, 13, 13, 13)" from Sleeve join, ending with a WS row, increase 1 st at middle of Back—206 (230, 254, 278, 302, 326) sts. Do not break yarn; leave sts on needle and set aside.

FINISHING

Note: If you prefer to knit rather than crochet the Front Placket and Neckbands, CO 10 sts and work in a non-curling st pattern such as Seed st or Garter st for the lengths given below, dividing the sts in half as instructed for the crochet piece.

Front Placket and Neckbands

With RS facing, using crochet hook, ch 10. Beginning in first st from hook, work single crochet (sc) (see Special Techniques, page 156) in each ch; work even until piece measures 11 ½ (11 ½, 11 ¾, 12, 12, 12)" from the beginning.

NEXT ROW: Continuing in sc, work 5 sc, turn. Working on these 5 sts only, work even for 17 (17 ¾, 18, 18 ½, 19 ¼, 20)", or until piece measures long enough to reach from base of Front neck shaping to center Back neck, allowing enough ease so that Neckband will lay flat when worn. Fasten off but do not break yarn; set aside. Join a second ball of yarn to 5 sts remaining at top of Placket; work as for first side. Pin two ends together. Sew Placket to Fronts, ending at base of Front neck shaping. Pin each Neckband to Fronts and try on sweater; adjust length of Neckbands if necessary. Sew edges of Neckbands to Fronts, being careful to maintain ease.

BOTTOM BAND

With RS facing, rejoin yarn to bottom edge of Left Front. Knit to end, pick up and knit 6 sts in bottom of Placket—212 (236, 260, 284, 308, 332) sts. Begin 1x1 Rib; work even for 1 ½". BO all sts in pattern.

Weave in ends. Block as desired.

blooming peonies
sweater

For this sweater, I combined a brick-colored linen and a vivid fuchsia mohair to produce an ultra-soft kimono that reminds me of a bouquet of fresh peonies. For the collar and cuffs, I combined the mohair with a comfy, like-colored sock yarn, and I love the depth of color it produced.

STITCH PATTERN

1x1 Rib
(multiple of 2 sts; 1-rnd repeat)
ALL RNDS: *K1, p1; repeat from * to end.

BACK/SLEEVES

Using crochet hook, waste yarn, and Provisional CO (see Special Techniques, page 155), CO 195 (206, 217, 228, 239, 250) sts. Change to larger circ needle and 1 strand each of A and B held together. Begin St st, beginning with a knit row; work even for 2 rows.

NEXT ROW (RS): K78 (82, 87, 92, 97, 102), pm, k39 (42, 43, 44, 45, 46), pm, knit to end.

Shape Shoulders/Sleeves

Note: Shoulders are shaped using short rows (see Special Techniques, page 153).
SHORT ROWS 1 (WS) AND 2: Work to second marker, sm, work 4 (3, 3, 3, 3, 3) sts, wrp-t.

SHORT ROWS 3–30 (32, 34, 36, 38, 40): Work to wrapped st from row before previous row, hide wrap, work 4 sts, wrp-t.

Work even across all sts, hiding remaining wraps as you come to them, until piece measures 6 (6, 6, 6¼, 6¼, 6½)" along side edge, ending with a RS row. Break yarn and transfer first and last 50 (51, 52, 53, 54, 55) sts to waste

sizes
Small (Medium, Large, 1X-Large, 2X-Large, 3X-Large)

finished measurements
32½ (36½, 40½, 44½, 48½, 52½)" bust

yarn
Shibui Knits Silk Cloud (60% kid mohair / 40% silk; 330 yards / 25 grams): 3 (4, 4, 4, 5, 5) hanks Raspberry (A)

Shibui Knits Linen (100% linen; 246 yards / 50 grams): 3 (4, 4, 4, 5, 5) hanks Brick (B)

Shibui Sock (100% superwash merino wool; 191 yards / 50 grams) 1 (2, 2, 2, 2, 2) hank(s) Peony (C)

needles
One 29" (70 cm) long circular (circ) needle size US 8 (5 mm)

One 24" (60 cm) long circular needle size US 4 (3.5 mm)

One set of five double-pointed needles (dpn) size US 4 (3.5 mm)

Change needle size if necessary to obtain correct gauge.

notions
Crochet hook size US H/8 (5 mm); waste yarn; stitch markers; removable stitch markers

gauge
18 sts and 24 rows = 4" (10 cm) in Stockinette stitch (St st), using larger needles and 1 strand each of A and B held together

23 sts and 32 rows = 4" (10 cm) in 1x1 Rib, using smaller needles and 1 strand each of A and C held together, slightly stretched

yarn for Sleeves; transfer remaining 95 (104, 113, 122, 131, 140) sts to separate waste yarn for Body.

FRONT/SLEEVES

With RS facing, carefully unravel Provisional CO and place sts on longer circ needle for Front.

Shape Shoulders/Sleeves and Neck

Note: Shoulders and neck are shaped at the same time; please read entire section through before beginning.

NEXT ROW (RS): Rejoin yarn; pm to mark Sleeve edge, k78 (82, 87, 92, 97, 102), pm to mark top of shoulder, join a second ball of yarn, BO 39 (42, 43, 44, 45, 46) sts for Back neck, knit to end—78 (82, 87, 92, 97, 102) sts remain each side for Shoulders/Sleeves. Working BOTH SIDES AT THE SAME TIME, using separate balls of yarn, work even in St st for 2 rows. Shape Shoulders/Sleeves as for Back. AT THE SAME TIME, when piece measures 5 (5, 5 1/4, 5 1/4, 5 1/2, 5 1/2)" from top-of-shoulder marker, begin neck shaping as follows:

Shape Neck

INCREASE ROW (RS): Continuing to shape Shoulders/Sleeves as established if necessary, increase 1 st at each neck edge this row, then every other row once, as follows: On right side, knit to last 2 sts, M1-R, k2; on left side, k2, M1-L, knit to end—80 (84, 89, 94, 99, 104) sts each Shoulder/Sleeve. Purl 1 row.

Join Fronts

NEXT ROW (RS): Knit across Right Front sts, CO 35 (38, 39, 40, 41, 42) sts for center neck, knit across Left Front sts, breaking second ball of yarn—195 (206, 217, 228, 239, 250) sts. Work even until piece measures 6 (6, 6, 6 1/4,

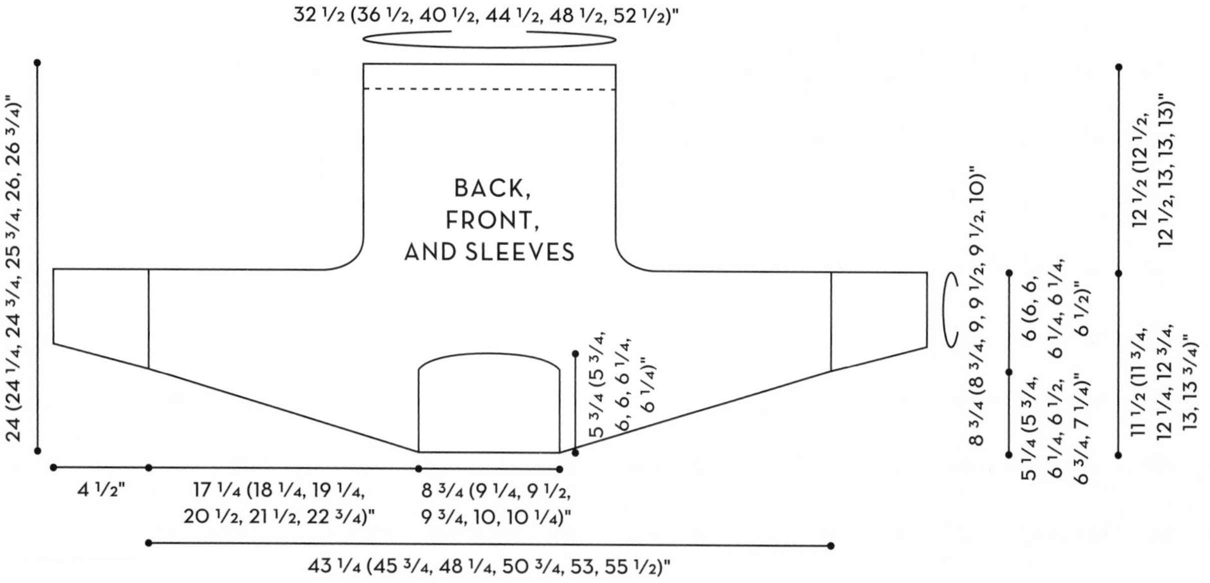
32 1/2 (36 1/2, 40 1/2, 44 1/2, 48 1/2, 52 1/2)"
BACK, FRONT, AND SLEEVES
24 (24 1/4, 24 3/4, 25 3/4, 26, 26 3/4)"
5 3/4 (5 3/4, 6, 6 1/4, 6 1/4)"
8 3/4 (8 3/4, 9, 9 1/2, 9 1/2, 10)"
6 (6, 6, 6 1/4, 6 1/4, 6 1/2)"
5 1/4 (5 3/4, 6 1/4, 6 1/2, 6 3/4, 7 1/4)"
12 1/2 (12 1/2, 12 1/2, 13, 13, 13)"
11 1/2 (11 3/4, 12 1/4, 12 3/4, 13, 13 3/4)"
4 1/2"
17 1/4 (18 1/4, 19 1/4, 20 1/2, 21 1/2, 22 3/4)"
8 3/4 (9 1/4, 9 1/2, 9 3/4, 10, 10 1/4)"
43 1/4 (45 3/4, 48 1/4, 50 3/4, 53, 55 1/2)"

6 ¼, 6 ½)" from Sleeve edge marker, ending with a RS row. Break yarn and transfer first and last 50 (51, 52, 53, 54, 55) sts to waste yarn for Sleeves. Leave remaining 95 (104, 113, 122, 131, 140) sts on needle for Body.

BODY

Join Back and Fronts

NEXT ROW (RS): Work across Front sts, pm for side, work across Back sts from waste yarn—190 (208, 226, 244, 262, 280) sts. Join for working in the rnd; pm for beginning of rnd. Work to last 2 sts.

Shape Armholes

Note: Each armhole shaping rnd begins 2 sts before beginning-of-rnd marker.

NEXT RND: Decrease 4 sts this rnd, then every rnd 10 times, working decreases on last 2 sts of rnd and first 2 sts of next rnd, as follows: [K2tog, sm, k1, ssk, knit to 2 sts before next marker] twice, knit to end—146 (164, 182, 200, 218, 236) sts remain. Work even until piece measures 11 (11, 11, 11½, 11½, 11½)" from beginning of armhole shaping. Change to smaller needles, 1 strand each of A and C held together, and 1x1 Rib; work even for 1½". BO all sts in pattern.

FINISHING

Using Kitchener Stitch (see Special Techniques, page 152) and 1 strand each of A and B held together, graft bottom edges of Sleeves. Close gaps at armholes.

Collar

With RS facing, using smaller circular needle and 1 strand each of A and C held together, and beginning at right shoulder, pick up and knit 39 (42, 43, 44, 45, 46) sts along Back Neck, 40 (40, 41, 41, 43, 43) sts to center Front neck, 35 (38, 39, 40, 41, 42) sts from CO sts, then 40 (40, 41, 41, 43, 43) sts to Back neck—154 (160, 164, 166, 172, 174) sts. Join for working in the rnd; pm for beginning of rnd. Begin 1x1 Rib; work even for 1½". BO all sts in pattern.

Cuffs

With RS facing, using dpns and 1 strand each of A and C held together, and beginning at Kitchener st graft (bottom edge of Sleeve), pick up and knit 60 (60, 62, 64, 64, 68) sts around Sleeve edge. Join for working in the rnd; place removable marker on first st of rnd for beginning of rnd. Begin 1x1 Rib; work even for ¾", ending 1 st before beginning of next rnd.

Shape Cuff

Note: Each cuff shaping rnd begins 1 st before beginning-of-rnd marker.

DECREASE RND: Decrease 2 sts this rnd, then every 6 rnds four times, working decrease on last st of rnd and first 2 sts of next rnd, as follows: Work 3 sts together (last st of rnd together with first 2 sts of next rnd; work p3tog if first st is a purl st, or sk2p if first st is a knit st), work to end; reposition beginning-of-rnd marker to before decreased st—50 (50, 52, 54, 54, 58) sts remain. Work even until piece measures 4½" from pick-up rnd. BO all sts in pattern.

Weave in all ends. Block as desired.

good things cardigan

Stitch patterns can help personalize your work in meaningful ways, and my goal for this cardigan was to bring together an assortment of stitches that referenced good things and made me smile. As a longtime fan of the country music I grew up listening to in the 1970s (including George Jones, Kris Kristofferson, and Willie Nelson), Walker's Banjo and Mutton-Chop Cables (both from her *Second Treasury of Knitting Patterns*) stood out and felt right and true. The pattern I chose for the button band reminds me of coffee beans and provides an ode of sorts to a kind barista in my neighborhood who introduced me to the Chemex method of making coffee and who often served me the perfect cup on days when my book's deadlines felt especially daunting.

ABBREVIATIONS

1/3 LT: Slip next st to cn, hold to front, p2, k1, k1 from cn.

1/3 RT: Slip 3 sts to cn, hold to back, k1, [k1, p2] from cn.

4/4 RC-p: Slip 4 sts to cn, hold to back, p4, k4 from cn.

4/4 LC-p: Slip 4 sts to cn, hold to front, k4, p4 from cn.

STL (seeded twist left): Slip 1 st to cn, hold to front, k1, p1, k1, [k1] from cn.

STR (seeded twist right): Slip 3 sts to cn, hold to back, k1, [p1, k1, p1] from cn.

sizes
X-Small (Small, Medium, Large, 1X-Large, 2X-Large)

finished measurements
31½ (35½, 40, 44, 48¼, 52¼)" chest, buttoned

yarn
Brooklyn Tweed Shelter (100% wool; 140 yards / 50 grams): 8 (9, 10, 11, 13, 13) hanks #07 Thistle

needles
One 29" (70 cm) long or longer circular (circ) needle size US 7 (4.5 mm)

One 16" (40 cm) long circular needle size US 7 (4.5 mm)

One set of five double-pointed needles (dpn) size US 7 (4.5 mm)

Change needle size if necessary to obtain correct gauge.

notions
Crochet hook size US F/5 (3.75 mm); waste yarn; stitch markers; cable needle; nine ½"-wide buttons

gauge
24½ sts and 29 rows = 4" (10 cm) over Mutton-Chop Cables

20 sts and 29 rows = 4" (10 cm) in Garter st (knit very row)

STITCH PATTERNS

Banjo Cable Flat (see Chart, page 112)
(panel of 12 sts; 16-row repeat)

ROW 1 (WS): K4, p4, k4.

ROW 2: P4, k4, p4.

ROW 3: K4, p1, slip 2 wyif, p1, k4.

ROW 4: P2, STR, STL, p2.

ROWS 5, 7, AND 9: K2, [p1, k1] 3 times, p2, k2.

ROWS 6, 8, 10: P2, [k1, p1] 3 times, k2, p2.

ROW 11: K2, slip 1 wyif, [k1, p1] 3 times, slip 1 wyif, k2.

ROW 12: P2, 1/3 LT, 1/3 RT, p2.

ROWS 13-16: Repeat Rows 1 and 2.

Repeat Rows 1-16 for Banjo Cable Flat.

Banjo Cable in the Rnd (see Chart, page 112)
(panel of 12 sts; 16-rnd repeat)

RNDS 1 AND 2: P4, k4, p4.

RND 3: P4, k1, slip 2 wyib, k1, p4.

RND 4: P2, STR, STL, p2.

RNDS 5, 7, AND 9: P2, k2, [k1, p1] 3 times, p2.

RNDS 6, 8, 10: P2, [k1, p1] 3 times, k2, p2.

RND 11: P2, slip 1 wyib, [k1, p1] 3 times, slip 1 wyib, p2.

RND 12: P2, 1/3 LT, 1/3 RT, p2.

RNDS 13-16: Repeat Rnd 1.

Repeat Rnds 1-16 for Banjo Cable in the Rnd.

Mutton-Chop Cables Flat (see Chart, page 112)
(multiple of 20 sts + 2; 10-row repeat)

ROWS 1, 3 AND 9 (WS): K2, *p8, k2; repeat from * to end.

ROWS 2 AND 8: *K10, p2, k8; repeat from * to last 2 sts, k2.

ROW 4: *K2, 4/4 RC-p, p2, 4/4 LC-p; repeat from * to last 2 sts, k2.

ROWS 5 AND 7: K2, *k4, p4, k2, p4, k6; repeat from * to end.

ROW 6: *K2, p4, k4, p2, k4, p4; repeat from * to last 2 sts, k2.

ROW 10: Repeat Row 2.

Repeat Rows 1-10 for Mutton-Chop Cables Flat.

Mutton-Chop Cables in the Rnd (see Chart, page 112)
(panel of 22 sts; 10-rnd repeat)

RNDS 1, 3, AND 9: P2, [k8, p2] twice.

RNDS 2 AND 8: K10, p2, k10.

RND 4: K2, 4/4 RC-p, p2, 4/4 LC-p, k2.

RNDS 5 AND 7: P6, k4, p2, k4, p6.

RND 6: K2, p4, k4, p2, k4, p4, k2.

RND 10: Repeat Rnd 2.

Repeat Rnds 1-10 for Mutton-Chop Cables in the Rnd.

2x2 Rib Flat
(multiple of 4 sts + 2; 1-row repeat)

ROW 1 (RS): P2, *k2, p2; repeat from * to end.

ROW 2: Knit the knit sts and purl the purl sts as they face you.

Repeat Row 2 for 2x2 Rib Flat.

2x2 Rib in the Rnd
(multiple of 4 sts; 1-rnd repeat)

ALL RNDS: *K2, p2; repeat from * to end.

Bramble Stitch
(multiple of 4 sts; 4-row repeat)

ROW 1 (WS): K2, *[k1, p1, k1] into next st, p3tog; repeat from * to last 2 sts, k2.

ROW 2: Purl.

ROW 3: K2, *p3tog, [k1, p1, k1] into next st; repeat from * to last 2 sts, k2.

ROW 4: Purl.

Repeat Rows 1-4 for Bramble Stitch.

BACK

Using crochet hook, waste yarn, and Provisional CO (see Special Techniques, page 155), CO 82 (82, 102, 102, 122, 122) sts. Change to longer circ needle and working yarn. Begin Mutton-Chop Cables Flat; work even until piece measures 9 (9¼, 9¾, 10¼, 10¾, 11)" from the beginning, ending with a WS row; make note of last row worked. Break yarn, transfer sts to waste yarn, and set aside.

FRONTS

With WS facing, carefully unravel Provisional CO and place sts on longer circ needle for Front. Mark armhole edge for top of armhole.

NEXT ROW (WS): Rejoin yarn; work 22 (22, 32, 32, 32, 32) sts in Mutton-Chop Cables Flat from Chart, beginning with st 22, join a second ball of yarn, BO 38 (38, 38, 38, 58, 58) sts for Back neck, work in Mutton-Chop Cables Flat from Chart to end, beginning with st 22 (22, 12, 12, 12, 12). Working BOTH SIDES AT THE SAME TIME using separate balls of yarn, work even until piece measures 4 (4, 4, 4½, 4½, 4½)" from marker, ending with a WS row.

Shape Neck
NEXT ROW (RS): CO 12 (12, 12, 12, 22, 22) sts at each neck edge—34 (34, 44, 44, 54, 54) sts each side.

NEXT ROW: On Left Front, work in Mutton Chop Cables Flat to last 12 sts, work in Banjo Cable Flat to end; on Right Front, work 12 sts in Banjo

BANJO CABLE

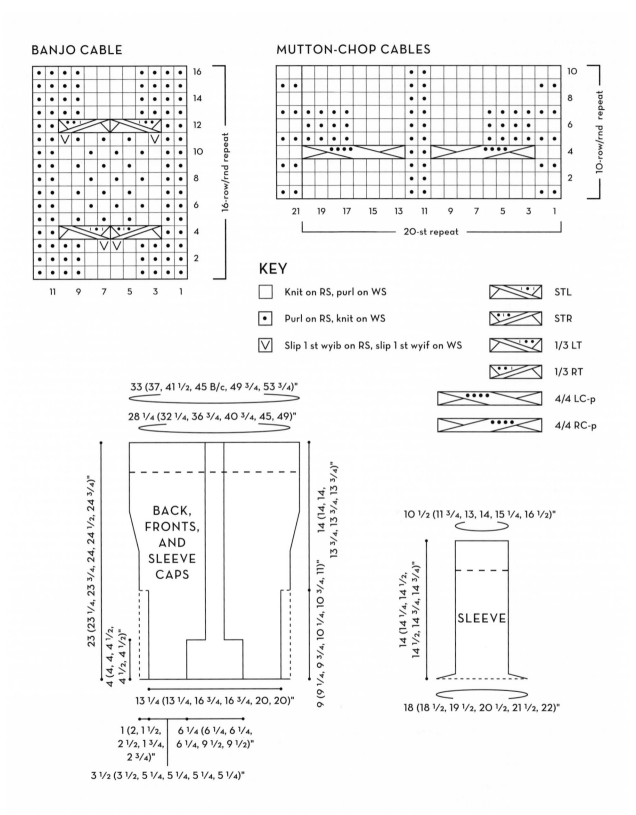

MUTTON-CHOP CABLES

20-st repeat

16-row/rnd repeat

10-row/rnd repeat

KEY

Knit on RS, purl on WS

• Purl on RS, knit on WS

V Slip 1 st wyib on RS, slip 1 st wyif on WS

STL

STR

1/3 LT

1/3 RT

4/4 LC-p

4/4 RC-p

33 (37, 41 ½, 45 B/c, 49 ¾, 53 ¾)"

28 ¼ (32 ¼, 36 ¾, 40 ¾, 45, 49)"

BACK, FRONTS, AND SLEEVE CAPS

23 (23 ¼, 23 ¾, 24, 24 ½, 24 ¾)"

4 (4, 4, 4 ½, 4 ½, 4 ½)"

9 ¼ (9 ¼, 9 ¾, 10 ¼, 10 ¾, 11)"

14 (14, 14, 13 ¾, 13 ¾, 13 ¾)"

13 ¼ (13 ¼, 16 ¾, 16 ¾, 20, 20)"

1 (2, 1 ½, 2 ½, 1 ¾, 2 ¾)"

6 ¼ (6 ¼, 6 ¼, 6 ¼, 9 ½, 9 ½)"

3 ½ (3 ½, 5 ¼, 5 ¼, 5 ¼, 5 ¼)"

10 ½ (11 ¾, 13, 14, 15 ¼, 16 ½)"

SLEEVE

14 (14 ¼, 14 ½, 14 ½, 14 ¾, 14 ¾)"

18 (18 ½, 19 ½, 20 ½, 21 ½, 22)"

Cable Flat, work in Mutton Chop Cables Flat to end. Work even until piece measures 9 (9¼, 9¾, 10¼, 10¾, 11)" from marker, ending with same row as for Back. Break yarn, transfer sts to waste yarn, and set aside.

SLEEVE CAP

With RS facing, using shorter circ needle, and beginning at base of right Back armhole, pick up and knit 90 (92, 98, 102, 108, 110) sts along armhole edge to base of Right Front armhole. Begin Garter st (knit every row); work even for 1 (2, 1½, 2½, 1¾, 2¾)", ending with a WS row. Break yarn, transfer sts to waste yarn, and set aside. Repeat for left armhole.

BODY

Join Back and Fronts

With RS facing, transfer Back sts, then Right Front sts to left-hand end of circ needle. Your sts should now be in the following order, from right to left, with RS facing: Left Front, Back, Right Front.

NEXT ROW (RS): Continuing in patterns as established, beginning with next row after last row worked on Fronts and Back, work across Left Front, pm, pick up and knit 5 (10, 7, 12, 9, 14) sts from Front side edge of Sleeve Cap, pm for side, pick up and knit 5 (10, 7, 12, 9, 14) sts from Back side edge of Sleeve Cap, pm, work across Back, pm, pick up and knit 5 (10, 7, 12, 9, 14) sts from Back side edge of Sleeve Cap, pm for side, pick up and knit 5 (10, 7, 12, 9, 14) sts from Front side edge of Sleeve Cap, pm, work across Right Front—170 (190, 218, 238, 266, 286) sts.

NEXT ROW: [Work to marker, work 10 (20, 14, 24, 18, 28) sts in Garter st, slipping side marker] twice, work to end. Continuing in patterns as established, work even until piece measures 4" from underarm, ending with a WS row.

Shape Hips

INCREASE ROW (RS): Increase 4 sts this row, then every 6 rows 5 times, as follows: [Work to 3 sts before side marker, M1, k6, slipping marker, M1] twice, work to end—194 (214, 242, 262, 290, 310) sts. Work even until piece measures 11 (11, 11, 10¾, 10¾, 10¾)" from underarm, ending with a WS row. Change to 2x2 Rib; work even for 3". BO all sts in pattern.

SLEEVES

With RS facing, transfer Sleeve Cap sts to shorter circ needle.

Shape Sleeve

DECREASE RND 1: Beginning at center of underarm, k0 (0, 4, 3, 6, 0), *k2 (3, 3, 4, 4, 7), k2tog; repeat from * to last 2 (2, 4, 3, 6, 2) sts, k2(2, 4, 3, 6, 2)—68 (74, 80, 86, 92, 98) sts remain. Join for working in the rnd; pm for beginning of rnd.

DECREASE RND 2: P2, [p0 (1, 2, 3, 4, 5), p2tog] 3 times, [k8, p2] twice, pm, work 12 sts in Banjo Cable in the Rnd, [p2, k8] twice, pm, [p2tog, p0 (1, 2, 3, 4, 5)] 3 times, p2—62 (68, 74, 80, 86, 92) sts remain.

NEXT RND: K3 (6, 9, 12, 15, 18), work Mutton-Chop Cables in the Rnd to next marker, beginning with Rnd 2 of pattern, work to next marker, work 22 sts in Mutton Chop Cables in the Rnd, beginning with Rnd 2 of pattern, k3 (6, 9, 12, 15, 18). Work even, working first and last 3 (6, 9, 12, 15, 18) sts of every rnd in Garter st (purl 1 rnd, knit 1 rnd), and remaining sts in patterns as established, until piece measures 11 (11¼, 11½, 11½, 11¾, 11¾)" from Sleeve Cap pick-up rnd. Change to 2x2 Rib in the Rnd; work even for 3". BO all sts in pattern.

FINISHING

Button Band

With RS facing, using longer circ needle and beginning at Left Front Neck edge, pick up and knit 3 sts for every 4 rows along Left Front, ending with a multiple of 4 sts. Begin Bramble st; work even for 1". Change to Garter st; work even for 1". BO all sts knitwise. Place markers for 9 buttons, the first ½" from bottom edge, the last ½" from top edge, and the remaining 7 evenly spaced between.

Buttonhole Band

Work as for Button Band, working buttonholes opposite markers when piece measures 1½" from pick-up row, as follows:

BUTTONHOLE ROW (RS): [Knit to marker, yo, k2tog] 9 times, knit to end. Complete as for Button Band. Sew buttons opposite buttonholes.

Neckband

With RS facing, using shorter circ needle and beginning at Right Front neck edge, pick up and knit 13 sts from Buttonhole Band, 1 st in each CO st and 3 sts for every 4 rows to Button Band, then 13 sts from Button Band. Knit 1 row. BO all sts knitwise.

Weave in ends. Block as desired.

robin's egg tunic

For this tunic, I chose an earthy pale blue shade of Louet Gems yarn and embraced the simplicity of Walker's square-set template (one she describes as "the easiest of all to knit" and which requires practically no shaping). This allowed me to focus on the subtlety and beauty of the King Charles Brocade (found in Walker's *Treasury of Knitting Patterns*), and to carefully shape the V-neck to follow its angle and lines. In the process, I discovered that the brocade benefits greatly from blocking and that either lightly steaming or wet-blocking the tunic when done goes a long way to help define the stitches and set them smoothly.

STITCH PATTERNS

King Charles Brocade Flat (see Chart, page 119)
(multiple of 12 sts + 1; 12-row repeat)

ROW 1 (RS): K1, *p1, k9, p1, k1; repeat from * to end.

ROW 2: *K1, p1, k1, p7, k1, p1; repeat from * to last st, k1.

ROW 3: K1, *p1, k1, p1, k5, [p1, k1] twice; repeat from * to end.

ROW 4: *P2, k1, p1, k1, p3, k1, p1, k1, p1; repeat from * to last st, p1.

ROW 5: K1, *k2, [p1, k1] 3 times, p1, k3; repeat from * to end.

ROW 6: P1, *p3, [k1, p1] twice, k1, p4; repeat from * to end.

ROW 7: K1, *k4, p1, k1, p1, k5; repeat from * to end.

ROW 8: Repeat Row 6.

ROW 9: Repeat Row 5.

ROW 10: Repeat Row 4.

ROW 11: Repeat Row 3.

ROW 12: Repeat Row 2.

Repeat Rows 1–12 for King Charles Brocade Flat.

sizes
X-Small (Small, Medium, Large, 1X-Large, 2X-Large)

finished measurements
32 (36, 40, 44, 48, 52)" bust

yarn
Louet Gems Sport Weight (100% merino wool; 225 yards / 100g) 6 (7, 7, 8, 9, 10) hanks #48 Aqua

needles
One 29" (70 cm) long circular (circ) needle US 3 (3.25 mm)

One 16" (40 cm) long circular needle US 3 (3.25 mm)

Change needle size if necessary to obtain correct gauge.

notions
Crochet hook size US D/3 (3.25 mm); waste yarn; stitch markers, including 2 removable markers

gauge
24 sts and 34 rows = 4" (10 cm) in King Charles Brocade

24 sts and 40 rows = 4" (10 cm) in Seed stitch)

King Charles Brocade in the Rnd (see Chart)
(multiple of 12 sts; 12-rnd repeat)

RND 1: *K5, p1, k1, p1, k4; repeat from * to end.

RND 2: *K4, [p1, k1] twice, p1, k3; repeat from * to end.

RND 3: *K3, [p1, k1] 3 times, p1, k2; repeat from * to end.

RND 4: *K2, p1, k1, p1, k3, p1, k1, p1, k1; repeat from * to end.

RND 5: *[K1, p1] twice, k5, p1, k1, p1; repeat from * to end.

RND 6: *P1, k1, p1, k7, p1, k1; repeat from * to end.

RND 7: *K1, p1, k9, p1; repeat from * to end.

RND 8: Repeat Rnd 6.

RND 9: Repeat Rnd 5.

RND 10: Repeat Rnd 4.

RND 11: Repeat Rnd 3.

RND 12: Repeat Rnd 2.

Repeat Rnds 1-12 for King Charles Brocade in the Rnd.

Seed Stitch Flat
(even number of sts; 1-row repeat)

ROW 1 (RS): *K1, p1: repeat from * to end.

ROW 2: Knit the purl sts and purl the knit sts as they face you.

Repeat Row 2 for Seed Stitch Flat.

Seed Stitch in the Rnd
(odd number of sts; 1-rnd repeat)

RND 1: K1, *p1, k1; repeat from * to end.

RND 2: Knit the purl sts and purl the knit sts as they face you.

Repeat Rnd 2 for Seed Stitch in the Rnd.

BACK

Using crochet hook, waste yarn, and Provisional CO (see Special Techniques, page 155), CO 85 (85, 97, 97, 109, 121) sts. Change to working yarn and longer circ needle. Begin King Charles Brocade Flat; work even until piece measures 9 (9 ¼, 9 ¾, 10 ¼, 10 ¾, 10 ¾)" from the beginning, ending with a WS row. Make note of last row worked. Break yarn, transfer sts to waste yarn, and set aside.

FRONT

With RS facing, carefully unravel Provisional CO and place sts on longer circ needle for Front. Mark armhole edge for top of armhole.

NEW ROW (RS): Work 13 (13, 13, 13, 13, 25) sts in King Charles Brocade Flat, work 0 (0, 3, 3, 6, 0) sts in St st, join a second ball of yarn, BO 59 (59, 65, 65, 71, 71) sts for Back neck, work 0 (0, 3, 3, 6, 0) sts in St st, work in King Charles Brocade to end. Working BOTH SIDES AT THE SAME TIME using separate balls of yarn, work even for 11 rows.

KING CHARLES BROCADE
FLAT

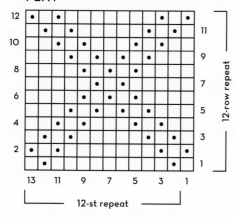

12-row repeat

12-st repeat

KING CHARLES BROCADE
IN THE RND

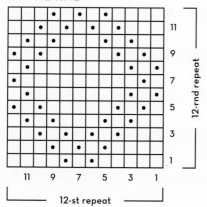

12-rnd repeat

12-st repeat

KEY

☐ Knit on RS, purl on WS.

⊡ Purl on RS, knit on WS.

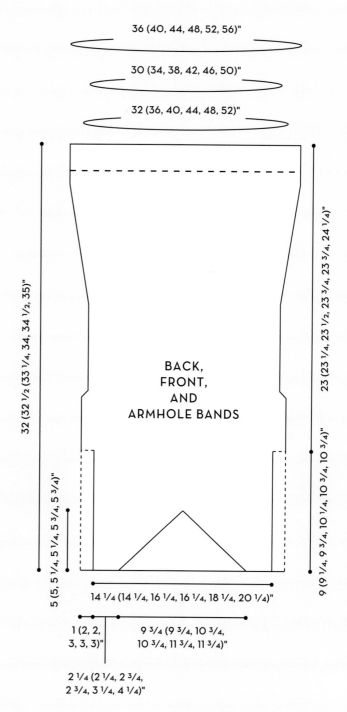

36 (40, 44, 48, 52, 56)"

30 (34, 38, 42, 46, 50)"

32 (36, 40, 44, 48, 52)"

BACK,
FRONT,
AND
ARMHOLE BANDS

32 (32 ½ (33 ¼, 34, 34 ½, 35)"

23 (23 ¼, 23 ½, 23 ¾, 23 ¾, 24 ¼)"

9 (9 ¼, 9 ¾, 10 ¼, 10 ¾, 10 ¾)"

5 (5, 5 ¼, 5 ¼, 5 ¾, 5 ¾)"

14 ¼ (14 ¼, 16 ¼, 16 ¼, 18 ¼, 20 ¼)"

1 (2, 2,
3, 3, 3)"

9 ¾ (9 ¾, 10 ¾,
10 ¾, 11 ¾, 11 ¾)"

2 ¼ (2 ¼, 2 ¾,
2 ¾, 3 ¼, 4 ¼)"

SHAPING PANEL CHART

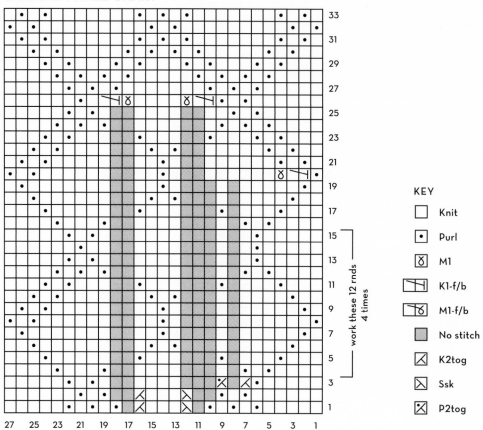

work these 12 rnds 4 times

KEY

☐ Knit

• Purl

⊗ M1

⊤ K1-f/b

⊤⊗ M1-f/b

▧ No stitch

⊠ K2tog

⊠ Ssk

⊠ P2tog

INCREASE PANEL CHART

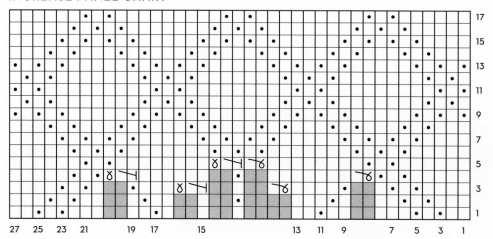

Shape Neck

NEXT ROW (RS): Increase 1 st at each neck edge this row, then every row 28 (28, 31, 32, 34, 34) times, working increased sts in King Charles Brocade Flat as they become available, as follows: RS rows: On right neck edge, work to last st, [k1, p1] into same st; on left neck edge, [k1, p1] into same st, work to end. WS rows: On left neck edge, work to end, CO 1 st; on right neck edge, CO 1 st, work to end—42 (42, 48, 48, 54, 60) sts each side. Work even for 1 row.

Join Fronts

NEXT ROW (RS): Work to end of Right Front, CO 1 st, work to end of Left Front—85 (85, 97, 97, 109, 121) sts. Work even until armhole measures same as for Back, ending with same row as for Back. Set aside, leaving sts on needle.

ARMHOLE BAND

With RS facing, using shorter circ needle and beginning at base of right Back armhole, pick up and knit approximately 2 sts for every 3 rows along armhole edge to base of right Front armhole. Begin Seed st Flat; work even for 1 (2, 2, 3, 3, 3)". BO all sts in pattern. Break yarn.

BODY

Join Back and Front

With RS facing, transfer Back sts to left-hand end of circ needle.

NEXT ROW (RS): Continuing in pattern as established, work across Front, beginning with next row after last row worked on Back and Front, pick up and knit 11 (23, 23, 35, 35, 35) sts from Front and Back side edges of Armhole Band, pm for side on center picked-up st, work across Back sts, pick up and knit 11 (23, 23, 35, 35, 35) sts from Back and Front side edges of Armhole Band, pm for side and beginning of rnd on center picked-up st—192 (216, 240, 264, 288, 312) sts. Join for working in the rnd. Change to King Charles Brocade in the Rnd, beginning with next rnd after last row worked; work even until piece measures approximately 4 (5, 4½, 5½, 5, 5)" from underarm, ending with Rnd 5 (11, 11, 5, 5, 5) of pattern, and ending 13 sts before marked st at beginning of rnd.

Shape Body

NEXT RND: Pm, work Shaping Panel Chart over next 27 sts, pm, work to 13 sts before next marked st, work Shaping Panel Chart over next 27 sts, pm, work to end—188 (212, 236, 260, 284, 308) sts remain. Continue to work Shaping Panel Chart between markers as established, working decreases and increases as indicated, until entire Chart is complete—192 (216, 240, 264, 288, 312) sts. Change to Increase Panel Chart, working increases as indicated, and work until Chart is complete—216 (240, 264, 288, 312, 336) sts. Work even until piece measures 21 (21¼, 21½, 21¾, 21¾, 22¼)" from underarm. Change to Seed st in the Rnd; work even for 2". BO all sts in pattern.

Weave in ends. Block as desired.

porcupine sweater

Walker's square-shaped dropped-shoulder template beckoned me to design a sweater with rich texture and color. I chose Louet's glorious Gems yarn in Teal and the intricate Porcupine stitch (from Walker's *A Second Treasury of Knitting Patterns*), finding that the raised shapes do indeed resemble the prickly creature's silhouette. The scalloped edges at the neckline were an unexpected and added bonus of working the sweater from the top down, and the slightly see-through nature of the stitch pattern offers creative layering opportunities.

ABBREVIATIONS

P2sp: P2tog, slip next st to right-hand needle knitwise, slip 2 sts from right-hand needle back to left-hand needle wyif, pass second st over first st, slip remaining st back to right-hand needle wyif (2 sts decreased).

STITCH PATTERNS

Porcupine Stitch Flat
(multiple of 12 sts + 4; 9-row repeat)

Note: Since this pattern has an odd number of rows, you will work Row 1 on a RS row the first time, then on a WS row the next time, continuing to alternate in this manner.

ROW 1: K2, *yo, k2tog; repeat from * to last 2 sts, k2.

ROWS 2 AND 4: K2, purl to last 2 sts, k2.

ROW 3: Knit.

ROWS 5 AND 8: K2, *sk2p, k4, yo, k1, yo, k4; repeat from * to last 2 sts, k2.

ROWS 6, 7 AND 9: K2, *p3tog, p4, yo, p1, yo, p4; repeat from * to last 2 sts, k2.
Repeat Rows 1-9 for Porcupine Stitch Flat.

sizes
X-Small (Small, Medium, Large, 1X-Large, 2X-Large, 3X-Large)

finished measurements
30 ¾ (34 ¼, 37 ¾, 41 ¼, 44 ½, 48, 51 ½)" bust

yarn
Louet Gems Sport Weight (100% merino wool; 225 yards / 100 grams): 5 (5, 6, 7, 7, 8, 9) hanks #54 Teal

needles
One 24" (60 cm) long circular (circ) needle size US 5 (3.75 mm)

One 16" (40 cm) long circular needle size US 5 (3.75 mm)

Change needle size if necessary to obtain correct gauge.

gauge
28 sts and 36 rows = 4" (10 cm) in Porcupine Stitch

notions
Crochet hook size US F/5 (3.75 mm); waste yarn; stitch markers; 2 yards thin, round elastic cord

Porcupine Stitch Half Repeat Right
(panel of 6 sts; 18-row repeat)

ROWS 1 AND 10: [Yo, k2tog] 3 times.

ROWS 2, 4, 11, AND 13: Purl.

ROWS 3 AND 12: Knit.

ROWS 5 AND 17: Skp, k4, yo.

ROWS 6 AND 16: P2tog, yo, p4.

ROWS 7, 9, AND 15: P2tog, p4, yo.

ROWS 8 AND 14: K2tog, yo, k4.

ROW 18: Repeat Row 6.

Repeat Rows 1-18 for Porcupine Stitch Half Repeat Right.

Porcupine Stitch Half Repeat Left
(panel of 6 sts; 18-row repeat)

ROWS 1 AND 10: [Yo, k2tog] 3 times.

ROWS 2, 4, 11, AND 13: Purl.

ROWS 3 AND 12: Knit.

ROWS 5 AND 17: K1, yo, k4.

ROWS 6 AND 16: P2tog, p4, yo.

ROWS 7, 9, AND 15: P2tog, yo, p4.

ROWS 8 AND 14: P2tog, k4, yo.

ROW 18: Repeat Row 6.

Repeat Rows 1-18 for Porcupine Stitch Half Repeat Left.

Porcupine Stitch in the Rnd (see Chart)
(multiple of 12 sts; 18-rnd repeat)

RND 1: *Yo, k2tog; repeat from * to end.

RNDS 2-4: Knit.

RND 5: *Sk2p, k4, yo, k1, yo, k4; repeat from * to end.

RND 6: *K4, yo, k1, yo, k4, k3tog; repeat from * to end.

RND 7: *P3tog, p4, yo, p1, yo, p4; repeat from * to end.

RND 8: *P4, yo, p1, yo, p4, p2sp; repeat from * to end.

RND 9: Repeat Rnd 7.

RND 10: *P2tog, yo; repeat from * to end.

RNDS 11-13: Purl.

RND 14: *P4, yo, p1, yo, p4, p2sp; repeat from * to end.

RND 15: *P3tog, p4, yo, p1, yo, p4; repeat from * to end.

RND 16: *K4, yo, k1, yo, k4, k3tog; repeat from * to end.

RND 17: *Sk2p, k4, yo, k1, yo, k4; repeat from * to end.

RND 18: *K4, yo, k1, yo, k4, k3tog; repeat from * to end.

Repeat Rows 1-18 for Porcupine Stitch in the Rnd.

BACK

Using crochet hook, waste yarn, and Provisional CO (see Special Techniques, page 155), CO 112 (124, 136, 148, 160, 172, 184) sts. Change to shorter circ needle and working yarn. Begin Porcupine Stitch Flat; work even until piece measures approximately 8 (8, 8, 9, 9, 10, 10)" from the beginning, ending with Row 2 (2, 2, 1, 1, 2, 2) of Porcupine Stitch Flat (ending on WS). Break yarn, leaving sts on the needle.

FRONT

With RS facing, carefully unravel Provisional CO and place sts on circ needle for Front. Mark armhole edge for top of armhole. Begin Porcupine Stitch Flat; work even for 1 row.

Shape Neck

NEXT ROW (WS): Work 28 (34, 40, 46, 52, 52, 58) sts, join a second ball of yarn, BO 56 (56, 56, 56, 56, 68, 68) sts for Back neck, work to end—28 (34, 40, 46, 52, 52, 58) sts remain each side for shoulders.

SIZES SMALL, LARGE, AND 3X-LARGE ONLY

On right neck edge, work in Porcupine Stitch Flat to last 8 sts before neck edge (ending before the last "k2" of pattern), work 6 sts in Porcupine Stitch Half Repeat Right, k2; on left neck edge, k2, work 6 sts in Porcupine Stitch Half Repeat Left, work in Porcupine Stitch Flat (beginning after the first "k2" of pattern) to end. Continue in this fashion, until sides of neck are joined.

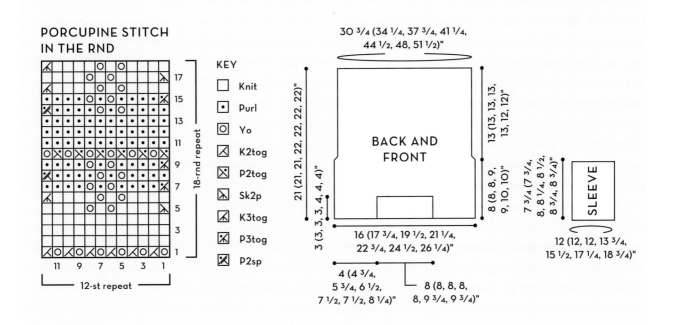

ALL SIZES

Working BOTH SIDES AT THE SAME TIME using separate balls of yarn, work even for approximately 3 (3, 3, 3, 4, 4, 4)" from marker, ending with Row 1 (1, 1, 1, 1, 2, 2, 2) of Porcupine Stitch Flat (ending on WS). Break yarn for left side.

NEXT ROW (RS): Work across Right Front, CO 56 (56, 56, 56, 56, 68, 68) sts for neck, work to end—112 (124, 136, 148, 160, 172, 184) sts. Work even in Porcupine Stitch Flat until piece measures approximately 8 (8, 8, 9, 9, 10, 10)" from marker, ending with Row 2 (2, 2, 1, 1, 2, 2) of Porcupine Stitch Flat (ending on WS).

BODY

Join Back and Front

*Work 3 sts together (k3tog if working on a knit row, p3tog if working on a purl row), work to last 3 sts of Front, work 3 sts together, pm, work 3 sts together, work to last 3 sts of Back, work 3 sts together—216 (240, 264, 288, 312, 336, 360) sts. Join for working in the rnd; pm for beginning of rnd. Change to Porcupine Stitch in the Rnd (from text or Chart), beginning with next st after last st worked for Front, and beginning with Rnd 4 (4, 4, 12, 12, 4, 4); work even until piece measures approximately 13 (13, 13, 13, 13, 12, 12)" from underarm, ending with Rnd 11 (11, 11, 11, 11, 2, 2) of Porcupine Stitch in the Rnd. BO all sts knitwise.

SLEEVES

With RS facing, using shorter circ needle and beginning at center of underarm, pick up and knit 84 (84, 84, 96, 108, 120, 132) sts evenly around armhole. Begin Porcupine Stitch in the Rnd (from text or Chart); work even until piece measures approximately 7¾ (7¾, 8, 8¼, 8½, 8¾, 8¾)" from underarm, ending with Rnd 16 (16, 18, 2, 4, 6, 6) of Porcupine Stitch. BO all sts knitwise.

FINISHING

With RS facing, using crochet hook, work 1 rnd single crochet (sc) (see Special Techniques, page 156) evenly around neckline, working 1 sc in each CO st and 1 st in every 3 rows.

With RS facing, using crochet hook, work 1 rnd sc around Sleeve edges. With RS facing, using crochet hook, work 1 rnd sc around and bottom edge, then holding elastic cord parallel to edge, work 1 rnd sc around bottom edge and cord (optional). Adjust elastic cord to desired measurements, tie in knot to secure, and weave ends into rnds of sc. Weave in all ends. Block as desired, being careful not to flatten st pattern.

fox in the snow

To chart the image on this sweater, I made the rookie mistake of using knitting graph paper and colored pencils, unaware that knitting design software now exists that would have made the process considerably easier and less time-consuming. As it was, however, my old-school tactics allowed me to frequently tape the chart to my studio wall while I was working and linger with the design. I could step away, see how the image was coming together, and make adjustments that helped add dimension and depth. If you're interested in working intarsia creations of your own, I encourage you to embrace Walker's advice with this dropped-shoulder template and "give your imagination free rein." Consider letting your yarn choice guide the images you select to depict as I did here. The moment I held a hank of Shibui's Heichi in Brownstone in my hands, I saw the striking colorings of a fox and everything else quickly fell into place.

STITCH PATTERNS

2x2 Rib Flat
(multiple of 4 sts + 2; 1-row repeat)
ROW 1 (RS): K2, *p2, k2; repeat from * to end.
ROW 2: Knit the knit sts and purl the purl sts as they face you.
Repeat Row 2 for 2x2 Rib Flat.

sizes
Small/Medium (Medium/Large, Large/ 1X-Large, 1X-Large/ 2X-Large)

finished measurements
39 (43, 47, 51)" bust

yarn
Shibui Knits Heichi (100% silk; 105 yards / 50 grams): 8 (9, 10, 10) hanks Column (MC); 2 hanks Brownstone (A); 1 hank each Steel (B), Tar (C), Caffeine (D), and Sidewalk (E)

needles
One 29" (70 cm) long or longer circular (circ) needle size US 6 (4 mm)

One 16" (40 cm) long circular needle size US 6 (4 mm)

One set of five double-pointed needles (dpn) size US 6 (4 mm)

Change needle size if necessary to obtain correct gauge.

notions
Crochet hook size US F/5 (3.75 mm); waste yarn; stitch markers

gauge
20 sts and 26 rows = 4" (10 cm) in Stockinette stitch (St st)

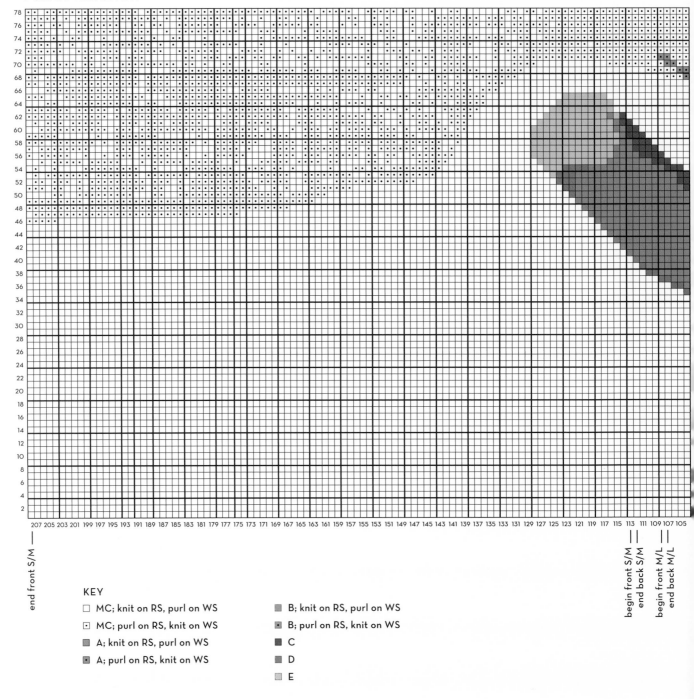

KEY

☐ MC; knit on RS, purl on WS

⊡ MC; purl on RS, knit on WS

■ A; knit on RS, purl on WS

▣ A; purl on RS, knit on WS

▩ B; knit on RS, purl on WS

▣ B; purl on RS, knit on WS

■ C

■ D

■ E

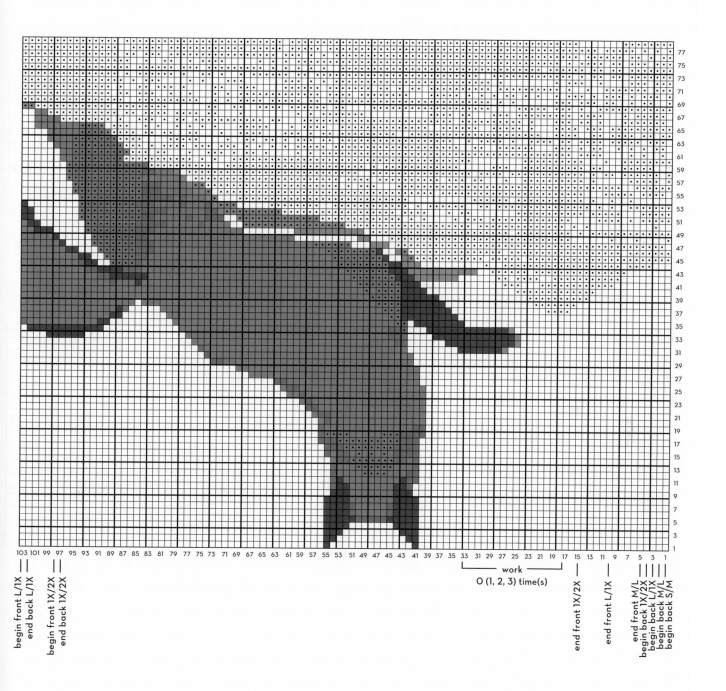

NOTE

✳ In order to make it easier to work the Fox Chart, which is worked in Intarsia (see Special Techniques, page 152), the Back and Front are worked back and forth. The Back is worked first from shoulder to bottom edge, then the Front is picked up from the Back shoulder and worked to bottom edge. The Fox Chart is intended to visually wrap around the entire body, with the Fox head centered in the front. Because of the size of the Chart, and the differing start and end points for the sizes, it was necessary to make one very large chart. Some sizes will have the Front and Back sts split between 2 ends of the Chart; you may find it easiest to photocopy the Chart, then cut and paste the pieces together so that you have the entire Front in one Chart, and the entire Back in a second Chart.

BACK

Using crochet hook, waste yarn, and Provisional CO (see Special Techniques, page 155), CO 98 (108, 118, 128) sts. Change to longer circ needle and MC. Begin St st, beginning with a purl row; work even until piece measures 8 (8½, 9, 9½)" from the beginning; pm at both sides for armholes. Work even for 1", ending with a WS row.

Begin Chart
NEXT ROW (RS): K1 (edge st; keep in St st), work Fox in the Snow Chart, beginning and ending as indicated in Chart for your size to last st, k1 (edge st, keep in St st). Work even until entire Chart is complete. Change to MC and 2x2 Rib Flat; work even for 2", dec 0 (2, 0, 2) sts evenly on first row—98 (106, 118, 126) sts. BO all sts in pattern.

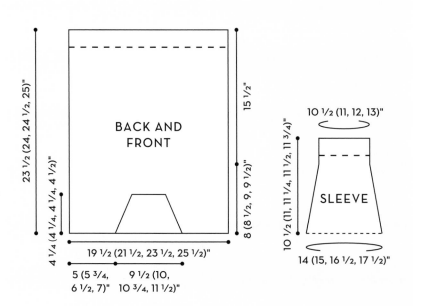

BACK AND FRONT

SLEEVE

23½ (24, 24½, 25)"

15½"

8 (8½, 9, 9½)"

4¼ (4¼, 4¼, 4½)"

19½ (21½, 23½, 25½)"

5 (5¾, 6½, 7)"

9½ (10, 10¾, 11½)"

10½ (11, 12, 13)"

10½ (11, 11¼, 11½, 11¾)"

14 (15, 16½, 17½)"

FRONT

With RS facing, carefully unravel Provisional CO and place sts on circ needle for Front. Mark armhole edge for top of armhole.

NEXT ROW (RS): Rejoin MC. K25 (29, 32, 35), join a second ball of yarn, BO 48 (50, 54, 58) sts for Back neck, knit to end. Working BOTH SIDES AT THE SAME TIME, using separate balls of yarn, purl 1 row.

Shape Neck

INCREASE ROW (RS): Increase 1 st at each neck edge this row, then every other row 12 (12, 12, 13) times, as follows: On right neck edge, knit to last 2 sts, M1-R, k2; on left neck edge, k2, M1-L, knit to end—38 (42, 45, 49) sts each side. Purl 1 row.

Join Fronts

NEXT ROW (RS): Knit across right Front sts, CO 11 (12, 14, 15) sts, pm, CO 11 (12, 14, 15) sts, knit across left Front sts—98 (108, 118, 128) sts. Continuing in St st, work even until piece measures 8 (8½, 9, 9½)" from top-of-armhole marker, ending with a WS row; pm at both sides for armholes. Work even for 1", ending with a WS row. Complete as for Back. Sew side seams from bottom edge to markers.

SLEEVES

Note: Change to dpns when necessary for number of sts on needle.

With RS facing, using shorter circ needle and MC, and beginning at center of underarm, pick up and knit 70 (76, 82, 88) sts evenly around armhole. Join for working in the rnd; pm for beginning of rnd. Begin St st; work even for 1", ending 2 sts before beginning of rnd.

Shape Sleeve

Note: Each Sleeve shaping rnd begins 2 sts before beginning-of-rnd marker.

DECREASE RND: Decrease 2 sts this rnd, every 6 (4, 4, 4) rnds 8 (3, 5, 7) times, then every 0 (6, 6, 6) rnds 0 (6, 5, 4) times, as follows: K2tog, sm, ssk, knit to end—52 (56, 60, 64) sts remain. Work even until piece measures 9 (9¼, 9½, 9¾)" from underarm. Change to 2x2 Rib in the Rnd; work even for 2". BO all sts in pattern.

FINISHING

Block as desired.

Neckband

With RS facing, using smaller circ needle and MC, and beginning at right shoulder, pick up and knit 1 st for every CO st and 2 sts for every 3 rows around neck opening. Join for working in the rnd; pm for beginning of rnd. Begin 2x2 Rib in the Rnd; work even for 5 rnds. BO all sts in pattern.

Weave in all ends.

holly berry hat

For this hat, I used short rows to create an asymmetrical front and the elegant Woven Transverse Herringbone Stitch (from Walker's *A Treasury of Knitting Patterns*) along the bottom back edge.

STITCH PATTERN

Woven Transverse Herringbone
(multiple of 4 sts + 2; 24-row repeat)

ROW 1 (RS): K2, *slip 2 wyif, k2; repeat from * to end.

ROW 2: P1, *slip 2 wyib, p2; repeat from * to last st, p1.

ROW 3: Slip 2 wyif, *k2, slip 2 wyif; repeat from * to end.

ROW 4: P3, *slip 2 wyib, p2; repeat from * to last 3 sts, slip 2 wyib, p1.

ROW 5–12: Repeat Rows 1–4.

ROW 13: Repeat Row 3.

ROW 14: Repeat Row 2.

ROW 15: Repeat Row 1.

ROW 16: Repeat Row 4.

ROWS 17–24: Repeat Rows 13–16.

CROWN

Using dpns, CO 8 sts. Distribute sts evenly among 4 dpns. Join for working in the rnd, being careful not to twist sts; pm for beginning of rnd.

Shape Crown
Note: Change to circ needle when there are enough sts to fit on the needle.

RND 1: *K1-f/b; repeat from * to end—16 sts.

finished measurements
22" head circumference

yarn
Jade Sapphire Mongolian Cashmere 2-Ply (100% cashmere; 400 yards / 55 grams): 1 hank #201 Seeing Red

needles
One 16" (40 cm) long circular (circ) needle size US 2 (2.75 mm)

One set of five double-pointed needles (dpn) size US 2 (2.75 mm)

Change needle size if necessary to obtain correct gauge.

notions
Crochet hook size US C/2 (2.75mm); waste yarn; stitch markers in 2 colors

gauge
28 sts and 40 rows = 4" (10 cm) in Stockinette stitch (St st)

RND 2: *K2, pm; repeat from * to last 2 sts, k2—7 markers placed in addition to beginning-of-rnd marker.

INCREASE RND 1: Increase 8 sts this rnd, then every other rnd 16 times, as follows: *K1-f/b, knit to marker, sm; repeat from * to end—152 sts. Knit 1 rnd.

INCREASE RND 2: [K1-f/b, knit to marker, sm] twice, knit to end—154 sts. Remove all markers except beginning-of-rnd marker.

NEXT RND: Work 60 sts, pm (color A), work 60 sts pm (color B), work to end.

Shape Body

Note: Body is shaped using short rows (see Special Techniques, page 153).

SHORT ROWS 1 (RS) AND 2: Change to working back and forth. Work to marker A, sm, work 4 sts, wrp-t.

SHORT ROWS 3-24: Work to wrapped st from row before previous row, hide wrap, work 4 sts, wrp-t.

SHORT ROW 25: Work to wrapped st from row before previous row, hide wrap, do not turn; you should be at marker B. Knit to end. Place next 60 sts on waste yarn for Front, turn—94 sts remain for Back.

Shape Back

SHORT ROW 1 (WS): Work 3 sts, wrp-t.

SHORT ROW 2: Knit to end.

SHORT ROW 3: Work to wrapped st from row before previous row, hide wrap, work 3 sts, wrp-t.

SHORT ROW 4: Knit to end.

SHORT ROWS 5-30: Repeat Short Rows 3 and 4. Knit to end. Work even in St st across all sts for 1", hiding remaining wrap as you come to it. Change to Woven Transverse Herringbone; work even for 24 rows. BO all sts.

FINISHING

With RS facing, using crochet hook, work 1 row single crochet (sc) (see Special Techniques, page 156) along BO edge.

Front Edging and Ties

With RS facing, using circ needle and beginning at left-hand corner of BO edge, pick up and knit 34 sts along left edge of Back, knit across 60 sts from waste yarn, pick up and knit 24 sts along right edge of Back—118 sts. Break yarn and set aside. Using dpns, work I-Cord 16" long (see Special Techniques, page 150).

NEXT ROW (RS): K3, k2tog-tbl (last st of I-Cord together with 1 st from circ needle); slide sts back to right-hand end of needle. Continue in this manner, working a plain (non-attached) row of I-Cord at each Front corner, until all sts from circ needle have been used. Continue working I-Cord for 16". BO all sts. Weave in ends on both Ties and tie knot in ends.

Thread CO tail onto tapestry needle and pull through 8 CO sts; pull tightly and secure.

Weave in ends. Block as desired.

stormy lake hat

I grew up in the Finger Lakes region of New York and the Celadon shade of Madelinetosh's Merino Light yarn reminds me of Seneca Lake moments before a storm. A simple sequence of cables helps add subtle texture, and the top-down construction makes adjusting the final length and fit a breeze.

ABBREVIATIONS

C6B: Slip 3 sts to cn, hold to back, k3, k3 from cn.

C6F: Slip 3 sts to cn, hold to front, k3, k3 from cn.

CROWN

CO 8 sts. Distribute sts evenly among 4 dpns. Join for working in the rnd, being careful not to twist sts; pm for beginning of rnd.

Shape Crown and Work Cable Pattern

Note: Crown shaping and cable pattern will be worked at the same time; please read entire section through before beginning. Change to circ needle when there are enough sts to fit on the needle.

INCREASE RND 1: *K1-f/b; repeat from * to end—16 sts.

NEXT RND: *K2, pm; repeat from * to last 2 sts, k2—7 markers placed in addition to beginning-of-rnd marker.

INCREASE RND 2: Increase 8 sts this rnd, then every other rnd 22 times, as follows: *K1-f/b, knit to marker, sm; repeat from * to end—200 sts (25 sts between markers). AT THE SAME TIME, work cable crosses on non-increase rnds, as follows:

When you have 9 sts between markers, *k3, C6F; repeat from * to end.

When you have 14 sts between markers, *k1, C6B, knit to marker; repeat from * to end.

finished measurements
22" circumference

yarn
Madelinetosh Tosh Merino Light (100% superwash merino wool; 420 yards / 100 grams): 1 hank Celadon

needles
One 16" (40cm) long circular (circ) needle size US 2 (2.75 mm)

One set of five double-pointed needles (dpn) size US 2 (2.75mm)

Change needle size if necessary to obtain correct gauge.

notions
Crochet hook size US C/2 (2.75 mm); stitch markers; cable needle; tapestry needle

gauge
28 sts and 40 rows = 4" (10 cm) in Stockinette stitch (St st)

When you have 20 sts between markers, *k10, C6F, knit to marker; repeat from * to end.

When you have 22 sts between markers, *C6B, knit to marker; repeat from * to end.

When you have 24 sts beween markers, *k9, C6F, knit to marker; repeat from * to end.

When you have 25 sts between markers, *C6B, knit to marker; repeat from * to end. Work even for 2 rnds.

NEXT RND: *K3, C6F, knit to marker; repeat from * to end. Knit 6 rnds.

NEXT RND: *K10, C6B, knit to marker; repeat from * to end. Knit 2 rnds.

NEXT RND: *C6F, k12, C6B, k1; repeat from * to end. Knit 4 rnds.

NEXT RND: *K7, C6F, knit to marker; repeat from * to end. Knit 2 rnds.

DECREASE RND 1: *K2, k2tog, k14, k2tog, knit to marker; repeat from * to end—184 sts remain. Knit 2 rnds.

NEXT RND: *K17, C6B; repeat from * to end. Knit 10 rnds.

DECREASE RND 2: *C6F, k4, k2tog, k5, k2tog, knit to marker; repeat from * to end—168 sts remain.

NEXT RND: *K10, C6B, knit to marker; repeat from * to end. Knit 2 rnds.

DECREASE RND 3: *K7, k2tog, knit to marker; repeat from * to end—160 sts remain. Knit 1 rnd.

DECREASE RND 4: *K10, k2tog, knit to marker; repeat from * to end—152 sts remain. BO all sts.

FINISHING

With RS facing, using crochet hook, work ½" single crochet (sc) (see Special Techniques, page 156) along bottom edge.

Thread CO tail onto tapestry needle and pull through 8 CO sts; pull tightly and secure.

Weave in ends. Block as desired.

appendix

basic design descriptions

Barbara Walker's book *Knitting from the Top* presents instructions for knitting garments in twelve basic designs from the top down, not by providing line-by-line pattern instructions but by outlining the necessary construction steps that empower knitters to create their own designs using their own measurements.

Armed with Walker's ideas, knitters are free to experiment, and even those following patterns (such as the ones I've created here) are easily able to make adjustments along the way to suit their individual shapes and styles.

Basic descriptions of Walker's twelve templates are listed below in an effort to help orient and give beginner knitters a useful starting point for understanding each design. I encourage knitters interested in creating their own garments from the top down, or in learning more about the infinite creative possibilities top-down knitting enables, to study and enjoy *Knitting from the Top* as I did. It remains an unparalleled sourcebook.

1   Classic Raglan Pullover

This design begins with stitches cast on for the yoke at the neck opening. The cast-on stitches are then divided into four sections—two sleeves and the front and back, separated by a raglan "seam." The piece is worked in the round, and the yoke is shaped by increasing one stitch on either side of the raglan "seam" every other row.

2   Classic Raglan Cardigan

Like the Pullover, stitches for this design are cast on for the yoke at the neck opening, but the stitches are then divided into five sections—two sleeves, the back, and two fronts. The piece is then worked back and forth, with yoke shaping worked as for the Pullover.

3   Seamless Cape

The Cape is worked as for the Cardigan, except that the stitches that would become the sleeves in the Cardigan instead become the shoulders and sides of the Cape.

4 Seamless Skirt

The Skirt begins with stitches cast on for the waistband. After the waistband is completed, stitches are increased at four or more points around the Skirt. These increases may be repeated at desired intervals to create a more or less fitted design.

5 Reversible Pants

The Pants begin with stitches cast on for the waistband. After the waistband is complete, stitches are increased on either side of the center front and back. Stitches are then cast on for the crotch to join the front and back, and each leg is worked separately. Because the shaping is essentially the same for the back and front, the Pants are reversible.

6 Sleeveless Sweater

The Sleeveless Sweater begins by using a provisional cast-on for the shoulders and back neck. The back is then worked from the shoulders down (using short rows to shape the shoulders), including armhole shaping, after which the stitches are set aside. The front is picked up from the provisional cast-on and worked to the armholes as well, including neck and armhole shaping. The front(s) and back are then joined and worked to the bottom edge, working in the round for a pullover, or back and forth for styles that open in the front.

7 Seamless Set-In Sleeve

This design is worked the same as for the Sleeveless Sweater, except that sleeves are picked up from the armholes and worked in the round to the cuffs, with short-row shaping for the sleeve caps.

8 Seamless Saddle Shoulder

This design begins with a left and right saddle, which form the shoulders of the sweater; stitches are picked up along one edge of each saddle, with stitches cast on between the saddles for the front neck. The front is worked to the armholes, including armhole shaping, then the stitches are set aside. The back is picked up from the opposite edge of the saddles and worked down through the armhole shaping. Front and back are joined and worked in the round to the bottom edge. Sleeves are picked up from the armhole edge (including from the live saddle stitches) and worked in the round to the cuffs.

9　Kimono Sleeve

For this design, stitches are cast on provisionally for the entire width of the back, from cuff to cuff. The top of the sleeve and shoulder is shaped using short rows. The back is worked to the end of the cuff, then the underside of the sleeve is shaped to the base of the armholes, and the stitches are set aside. The front is picked up from the provisional cast-on and worked to the base of the armholes as well, shaping the sleeves, shoulders, and neck as you go. Front and back are joined and worked in the round to the bottom edge.

10　Square Set or Peasant Sleeve

The back begins using a provisional cast-on for the shoulders and back neck. The back is worked from the shoulders down to the base of the armhole, with no armhole shaping, after which the stiches are set aside. The front is picked up from the provisional cast-on and worked to the base of the armholes as well, including neck shaping. Stitches are picked up for the sleeve caps (or armhole bands if the piece is sleeveless), worked to the indicated length, then set aside. The front(s) and back are joined and stitches are picked up at the side edges of the sleeve caps/armhole bands, then the body is worked to the bottom edge, working in the round for a pullover, and back and forth for a cardigan.

11　Dropped Shoulder Ski Sweater

The back begins using a provisional cast-on for the dropped shoulders and back neck. The back is worked from the shoulders down to the base of the armhole, with no armhole shaping, after which the stiches are set aside. The front is picked up from the provisional cast-on and worked to the base of the armholes as well, including neck shaping. The front and back are joined and worked in the round to the bottom edge. Sleeves are picked up from the armhole openings and worked in the round to the cuffs.

12　Classic Cap

Stitches are cast on for the top center of the cap, then doubled on the following round. The piece is divided into equal sections, and one stitch is increased per section until the desired number of stitches is reached. The cap is then worked even in rounds to the end.

abbreviations

BO   Bind off

Ch   Chain

Circ   Circular

Cn   Cable needle

CO   Cast on

Dpn(s)   Double-pointed needle(s)

K   Knit

K1-f/b   Knit into the front loop and back loop of same stitch to increase one stitch.

K1-f/b/f   Knit into the front loop, back loop, then front loop of the same stitch to increase two stitches.

K1-tbl   Knit one stitch through the back loop.

K2tog   Knit two stitches together.

K3tog   Knit three stitches together.

M1 or M1-L (make 1-left slanting)   With the tip of the left-hand needle inserted from front to back, lift the strand between the two needles onto the left-needle; knit the strand through the back loop.

M1-b/f (make 1 back and front)   With the tip of the left-hand needle inserted from front to back, lift the strand between the two needles onto the left-hand needle; knit the strand through the back loop, then the front loop to increase two stitches.

M1-f/b (make 1 front and back)   With the tip of the left-hand needle inserted from back to front, lift the strand between the two needles onto the left-hand needle; knit the strand through the front loop, then the back loop to increase two stitches.

M1-p-L (make 1 purlwise-left slanting)   With the tip of the left-hand needle inserted from front to back, lift the strand between the two needles onto the left-hand needle; purl the strand through the back loop to increase one stitch.

M1-p-R (make 1 purlwise-right slanting)   With the tip of the left-hand needle inserted from back to front, lift the strand between the two needles onto the left-hand needle; purl the strand through the front loop to increase one stitch.

M1-R (make 1-right slanting)   With the tip of the left-hand needle inserted from back to front, lift the strand between the two needles onto the left-hand needle; knit it through the front loop to increase one stitch.

P   Purl

P1-f/b   Purl into the front loop and back loop of the same stitch to increase one stitch.

P2tog   Purl two stitches together.

Pm   Place marker.

Rnd(s)   Round(s)

RS   Right side

Sc (single crochet)   Insert the hook into the next stitch and draw up a loop (two loops on the hook), yarn over and draw through both loops on the hook.

Skp (slip, knit, pass)   Slip the next stitch knitwise to the right-hand needle, k1, pass the slipped stitch over the knit stitch.

Sk2p (double decrease)   Slip the next stitch knitwise to the right-hand needle, k2tog, pass the slipped stitch over the stitch from the k2tog.

Sm   Slip marker

Ssk (slip, slip, knit)   Slip next two stitches to right-hand needle one at a time as if to knit; return them to left-hand needle one at a time in their new orientation; knit them together through the back loops.

St(s)   Stitch(es)

Tbl   Through the back loop

Tog   Together

Wrp-t   Wrap and turn (see Special Techniques: Short Row Shaping, page 153)

WS   Wrong side

Wyib   With yarn in back

Wyif   With yarn in front

Yo   Yarnover

special techniques

Applied I-Cord

Using a double-pointed needle, cast on or pick up the required number of sts; the working yarn will be at the left-hand side of the needle. *Transfer the needle with the sts to your left hand, bring the yarn around behind the work to the right-hand side; using a second double-pointed needle, knit the sts from right to left, pulling the yarn from left to right for the first st, pick up and knit 1 st from edge to which I-Cord will be applied; do not turn. Slide the sts to the opposite end of the needle, knit to last 2 sts, ssk; repeat from * around the entire edge to which the I-Cord is to be applied, working even rows between pick-up rows if necessary so that I-Cord is smooth.

Backstitch

Bring tapestry needle up from wrong side to right side through first hole (A), then take needle back to wrong side through next hole (B). Bring yarn back to right side through third hole (C), then back to wrong side through B. Continue in this manner, working from wrong side to right side in the empty hole beyond last hole worked, then going backward 1 hole to go from right side to wrong side.

Duplicate Stitch

Duplicate st is similar to Kitchener st, except it is used for decorative purposes instead of joining two pieces together. Thread a tapestry needle with chosen yarn and, leaving a tail to be woven in later, *bring the needle from WS to RS of work at the base of the st to be covered, pass the needle under both loops (the base of the st above) above the st to be covered; insert the needle into same place where you started (base of st), and pull yarn through to WS of work. Be sure that the new st is the same tension as the rest of the piece. Repeat from * for additional sts.

A good way to visualize the path of the yarn for Duplicate st is to work a swatch in Stockinette st using main color (MC) for three rows, work 1 row alternating MC and a contrasting color, then work two additional rows using MC only.

French Knot
See page 154.

Intarsia Colorwork Method

Use a separate length of yarn for each color section; you may wind yarn onto bobbins to make color changes easier. When changing colors, bring the new yarn up and to the right of the yarn just used to twist the yarns and prevent leaving a hole; do not carry colors not in use across the back of the work.

Kitchener Stitch

Using a blunt tapestry needle, thread a length of yarn approximately 4 times the length of the section to be joined. Hold the pieces to be joined wrong sides together, with the needles holding the sts parallel, both ends pointing to the right. Working from right to left, insert tapestry needle into first st on front needle as if to purl, pull yarn through, leaving st on needle; insert tapestry needle into first st on back needle as if to knit, pull yarn through, leaving st on needle; *insert tapestry needle into first st on front needle as if to knit, pull yarn through, remove st from needle; insert tapestry needle into next st on front needle as if to purl, pull yarn through, leave st on needle; insert tapestry needle into first st on back needle as if to purl, pull yarn through, remove st from needle; insert tapestry needle into next st on back needle as if to knit, pull yarn through, leave st on needle. Repeat from *, working 3 or 4 sts at a time, then go back and adjust tension to match the pieces being joined. When 1 st remains on each needle, cut yarn and pass through last 2 sts to fasten off.

Provisional Cast-On

See page 155.

Running Stitch

*Insert threaded needle from RS of fabric to WS and back to RS a few times, moving forward each time, then pull through to WS. Repeat from * for desired length of line.

Satin Stitch

Cover an area with closely spaced straight stitches as follows: Bring threaded needle from WS to RS of fabric at one edge of area to be covered. *At opposite edge of area, bring needle from RS to WS and back to RS, catching smallest possible bit of background fabric. Repeat from *, carefully tensioning the stitches so work lies flat without puckering.

Short Row Shaping

Work the number of sts specified in the instructions, wrap and turn (wrp-t) as follows:

To wrap a knit st, bring yarn to the front (purl position), slip the next st purlwise to the right-hand needle, bring yarn to the back of work, return the slipped st on the right-hand needle to the left-hand needle purlwise; turn, ready to work the next row, leaving the remaining sts unworked. To wrap a purl stitch, work as for wrapping a knit st, but bring yarn to the back (knit position) before slipping the stitch, and to the front after slipping the stitch.

When short rows are completed, or when working progressively longer short rows, work the wrap together with the wrapped st as you come to it as follows:

If st is to be worked as a knit st, insert the right-hand needle into the wrap, from below, then into the wrapped st; k2tog; if st to be worked is a purl st, insert needle into the wrapped st, then down into the wrap; p2tog. (Wrap may be lifted onto the left-hand needle, then worked together with the wrapped st if this is easier.)

Single Crochet (sc)

See page 156.

Whipped Running Stitch

Whipped running stitch is worked over a foundation of running stitches (see Running Stitch). After working the running stitch foundation, wrap a second thread around this foundation, without picking up any fabric.

Working Embroidery on Knitted Fabric

See page 157.

FRENCH KNOT

Thread the tapestry needle with no more than an arm's length of yarn. Bring the needle up from the wrong side at the spot where you wish to make the knot. *Note: You may bring the needle up through the middle of a strand of yarn in the knitted fabric, rather than next to one, as this will help your knot sit on the surface.* With the needle lying next to where the yarn comes out, wrap the yarn three or four times (two or three times for a smaller knot) tightly around the needle tip (**A** and **B**), keeping a tight grip as you wrap it. Hold the wrapped yarn in place with your finger as you bring the needle to the wrong side again, about ⅛" from where it came up last, pulling the rest of the working yarn through the knot. The knot sits on the surface.

To create a French knot in the center of a sequin, thread the tapestry needle and bring the needle up through the sequin to the right side of the work. Wrap the yarn as above (**A** and **B**), and push the needle down through the center of the sequin, holding the thread tight in your fingers (**C**). Pull the needle through the knot and sequin to the wrong side of the fabric and secure.

CREATING A FRENCH KNOT IN THE CENTER OF A SEQUIN

PROVISIONAL CAST-ON

There are a few different ways to work a provisional cast-on, although I find this one to be the easiest.

With a crochet hook and smooth waste yarn in a color that contrasts with your working yarn, work a crochet chain for the number of stitches needed for the cast-on, plus a few extra stitches to keep the end from unraveling.

Flip the chain so its backside (with the purl bumps) faces you. Insert the crochet hook through the back loops, and pull the working yarn through the loops and onto the hook (**A**). Once you have four or five stitches on your hook, slip them to your needle (**B**). (Note that a knitting needle can be used instead of a crochet hook to work the first row of a provisional cast-on—you can experiment and see which one works best for you.) Repeat until you have cast on as many stitches as you need. Change to the working yarn, and work as directed in the pattern.

When you are ready to unravel the provisional cast-on and work the opposite edge, carefully undo the first stitch of the crochet chain and pull the tail of the waste yarn. Load the live stitches onto your needle as they are released (**C**). Change to the working yarn and work as instructed in the opposite direction.

PROVISIONAL CAST-ON

 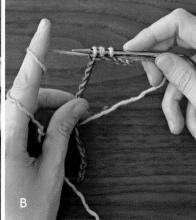 

SINGLE CROCHET

I typically work a row of single crochet along the edges of my designs because I like the finished look it provides.

To work single crochet (sc) along the cast-on, bound-off, or knitted edge of a garment, insert the hook into the first stitch in the row. Insert the hook into the next stitch, yarn over the hook, and draw the yarn through the stitch (you now have two loops on your hook). Yarn over the hook again and draw the yarn through both loops on the hook (**A**). You now have one loop on your hook and have completed one single crochet (**B**). Repeat the steps **A** and **B** in every knit stitch across the entire edge (**C**).

SINGLE CROCHET

If you are working only one row of single crochet, break the yarn at the end of the row and fasten off, leaving a 6" tail. If you are working another row of single crochet, yarn over the hook at the end of the first row, draw a loop through the remaining loop on your hook, turn your work, insert the hook under both loops of the first stitch (the last single crochet stitch you worked in the previous row), and work single crochet into each stitch across the row.

When working single crochet around a neckline, the sides of the neckline are worked along the edges of knitted rows. Work one single crochet in every other row (or two rows out of every three) to avoid bunching. When working across the cast-on or bound-off edge at the back neck, work single crochet in every stitch, as you would along the hem of a garment.

If you are working single crochet in the round, connect the first and last single crochet stitches by slipping your hook into the top of the first stitch worked; yarn over and pull a loop through the stitch and the loop on your hook to connect the stitches. Break the yarn and fasten off.

WORKING EMBROIDERY ON KNITTED FABRIC

After tracing your embroidery motif onto Solvy water-soluble stabilizer with gel pen, tape or pin it in place over your work. Being careful not to wrinkle the stabilizer, use a sewing needle and embroidery floss to embroider the image over the stabilizer.

Embroidering onto dense, knitted fabric is much easier to do with a piece of water-soluble stabilizer. Simply trace your motif onto the stabilizer, work the embroidery stitches, then easily dissolve the stabilizer with water.

sources

YARN

Be Sweet
www.besweetproducts.com

Blue Sky Alpacas, Inc.
www.blueskyalpacas.com

Brooklyn Tweed
www.brooklyntweed.net

Elsebeth Lavold
(distributed by Knitting Fever Inc.)
www.knittingfever.com

Jade Sapphire
www.jadesapphire.com

Jill Draper Makes Stuff
www.jilldraper.com

Louet North America
www.louet.com

Madelinetosh
www.madelinetosh.com

Malabrigo
www.malabrigoyarn.com

Rowan
www.knitrowan.com

Shelridge Farm
www.shelridge.com

Shibui
www.shibuiknits.com

SPECIALTY CRAFT SUPPLIES

Daytona Braids & Trimmings
www.daytonatrim.com

Leather Impact
(leather)
www.leatherimpact.com

Mood Fabrics
(leather)
www.moodfabrics.com

Tandy Leather Factory
(leather and rotary leather
hole punches)
www.tandyleatherfactory.com

recommended reading

BOOKS BY BARBARA G. WALKER

(all published by
Schoolhouse Press)

A Treasury of
Knitting Patterns

A Second Treasury of
Knitting Patterns

Charted Knitting Designs:
A Third Treasury of
Knitting Patterns

A Fourth Treasury of
Knitting Patterns

Knitting from the Top

acknowledgments

In creating the pieces for this book, I would meet with my editor, Melanie Falick, every few months (usually after completing a set of three or four items), go to her office to review the pieces, and talk with her about design, color, and fit. I could always count on Melanie for guidance and a pervasive sense of calm and curiosity during our conversations. Any extra care I might have taken (attaching a certain type of trim to an inside hem edge or tracking down buttons I especially liked) never went unnoticed by Melanie, and it was always incredibly rewarding and reassuring to me to receive her helpful thoughts and comments. There are no words to express how much her belief in my work has meant to me, or how much I value those meetings and our resulting friendship—I thank her sincerely.

My respect for Barbara Walker and her marvelous contributions to the field of knitting continues to deepen and grow stronger with every sweater I make. I thank her for the countless ways her work has inspired me and helped me to write this book.

I thank technical editor Sue McCain for her patience and skill working on my patterns. Time and again I felt in great hands with Sue, not only because she is meticulous and thorough, but because she's also thoughtful and caring and never once tired of going the extra mile to get everything just right. You are such a gem, Sue!

It was a special joy for me to get to know photographer Anna Williams and to realize what a gracious and warm person she is. And I am very grateful to gifted graphic designer Anna Christian for her beautiful work and care.

Thank you to Mason Adams, who organized an exciting and stress-free photo shoot with the kindest crew I could have hoped for, including Lorie Reilly, Jeff Denton, and Sabrina Rowe. Stylist Pamela Duncan Silver brought a wonderful sense of comfort and style to the photo shoot and I am thankful for the work she did.

On the home front, this book would have been considerably harder to complete (if not impossible) without the constant support of my mother, father, and sister. Their understanding, patience, and love have helped me weather many moments of doubt and have kept me feeling hopeful and grounded. I would also like to thank my dear and supportive uncle, George McGowan.

Throughout the writing of this book, I have been fortunate to have sympathetic (and brilliant) friends who consistently encouraged me and provided invaluable help and feedback, including Corinna Barsan, Heather Janbay, Thomas LeBien, Cecily Parks, Jonathan Lippincott, Michele Henjum, Susan Ervolina, Caryl McGinty, and Amy Benfer.

Esther and David Betten, the owners of the Argyle Yarn Shop in Brooklyn, New York, welcomed me into their beautiful shop many afternoons during the final stages of writing this book and provided support, friendship, and coffee. Thank you to both of them.

Grateful acknowledgment is also given to the people who generously sent me yarn and facilitated speedy deliveries, always mindful of my deadlines: Kristen Ford, Jill Draper, Katie Mayer, David Van Stralen, Jared Flood, Jane Saffir, Nadine Curtis, Tobias Feder, and Buffy Taylor.

And last but certainly not least, thank you to a lovely group of knitters, my troops, who all stepped up in the twelfth hour and helped me when I needed it most. Irina Lester was so dedicated and supportive that she wrote to me from her hospital room, hours after having given birth, just to assure me that she was still working on the Nokomis Cape and would not be late! She did the work beautifully. Amy Micallef was a bright star whose speed, workmanship, and ever-present smile proved a tremendous asset and lifesaver. Amy Detjen provided encouragement, worked on the Blooming Peonies sweater and introduced me to Julie Fisk. Julie Fisk knitted the body of the Fox in the Snow sweater with absolute perfection and converted my large hand-drawn chart into an elegant computer file. And Teva Durham kindly pitched in and always met my flurry and exhaustion with assurance and a knowing smile. My heartfelt thanks to all.

JULIANNA AND NOAH EHLERT

about the author

Kristina McGowan is a New York City–based knitwear designer. Her first book, *Modern Top-Down Knitting*, was published in 2010 by STC Craft, an imprint of ABRAMS.